D1521388

Praise for *Kentucky Basketball: Two Decades Behind the Scenes*

"Twenty years for Tom and Mike. Can you believe that? And more than half of that time working with me. It's been great fun and I know our fans are going to love reliving so many special moments that they have had a chance to witness from their courtside seat on the UK Sports Network. It's the perfect gift for any Wildcat fan."—John Calipari, head coach of the University of Kentucky Men's Basketball team

"Tom Leach and Mike Pratt bring their deep affection for Kentucky basketball to every broadcast. They are aware of the history of the program and its importance to the Big Blue Nation. Fans are blessed to have two of the best broadcasters share their love affair with the game."—Bill Raftery, CBS Sports

"Mike Pratt and Tom Leach are true blue Kentucky Wildcats who helped me and many others appreciate that Kentucky basketball is a lifestyle. They are two of the best broadcasters in the business. You will enjoy reading about Kentucky basketball from an announcer and from one of the best Wildcat players. I know you will learn a lot more about UK basketball and the Big Blue Nation."—Tubby Smith, former UK national champion coach and UK Hall of Famer

"For 20 years, Mike and Tom have honored Big Blue Nation and the game they love. They're the ultimate 'glue guys' for a fanbase with the highest standards. Just as you hear their passion for the Wildcats in every game broadcast, you'll feel it in these pages as you relive the excitement from their courtside seats."—Kaylee Hartung, ABC's *Good Morning America*

"I've done many basketball telecasts from Rupp Arena. I always enjoyed settling in to our broadcasting location and looking to my right and saying hello to Tom Leach and Mike Pratt, knowing that UK radio broadcasts were in the hands of superb and knowledgeable voices. Well done, guys."—Verne Lundquist, CBS Sports

"Has it really been 20 years since Tom Leach and Mike Pratt were paired up on the UK Basketball Network? It has, and that perfect match has resulted in a new book recounting their memories of the past 20 years of UK hoops. The first event I did on television was in December 1969, when UK scored 115 points in a rout of Kansas, led by Dan Issel and Mike Pratt. I followed Mike's career as a player, coach, and then broadcaster and even partnered with him on the telecast of a few games, years ago. He has been a success in everything he has done. As a native Kentuckian, Tom has been on my radar since he began his broadcasting career, and we have often discussed broadcasting techniques. That's why I have taken great pride in seeing Tom advance to be one of the finest radio play-by-play announcers in the nation. Given the excellent work turned in by Leach and Pratt together over the last 20 years, a book of their memories was a natural and is a must-read for Big Blue Nation."—Tom Hammond, NBC Sports

"Mike Pratt is a Lexington legend and an authority on Kentucky basketball. He and Tom Leach are one of the top radio teams in the country and this book feels like I'm listening to them chop it up on the air. It's a must-read for Wildcats fans young and old and a highly entertaining walk down memory lane! "—Ian Eagle, CBS Sports

"I got a small glimpse into the world of Big Blue Nation while covering the Kentucky Wildcats for ESPN from 2011 to 2016. I have read books, media guides, and heard hundreds of stories about the Cats, but nothing quite like *Kentucky Basketball: Two Decades Behind the Scenes*. Mike and Tom's perspective is one from the 'inside.' That historic buzzer beater? They were there. The Platoon System? They were there. The Calipari hiring? They were there! The coaches, the players, and the media have all changed over the last two decades, but Mike and Tom have been the constant, and now they are telling us how things really went down!"—Shannon Spake, Fox Sports

"When I watch a Kentucky basketball game, I always turn down the sound and listen to Tom and Mike on the radio. They focus on the game and don't make the broadcast about themselves. Their knowledge of the Wildcats program is greater than anyone's in media. I'm anxious to read all the great stories they have to tell."—Dan Issel, former UK basketball player and UK Hall of Famer

"You may have attended every UK game of the past two decades, and you may think you know it all, but you don't. You'll get the untold stories of tears and laughter, from Tayshaun's rocketing 'treys' against UNC to Jodie's 54-point night in K-town, from Billy Clyde's antics to Cal's title run, as only Tom & Mike can tell from their roles behind the mic and off the court. Must read."—Oscar Combs, founder of *The Cats Pause* and former UK Network pregame analyst

"For the last two decades, Mike Pratt and Tom Leach have had a front row seat for 'the greatest tradition in college basketball.' Their new book covers those 20 seasons, telling what happened and why—in the bright lights of game day and the stories behind the scenes. Their conversational style makes it an easy, engaging read and they add some great bonus material. It's a slam dunk for any UK fan!"—Mitch Barnhart, director of athletics at the University of Kentucky

"Since I grew up in Lexington and had the opportunity to play basketball all over the state of Kentucky during my high school years at Bryan Station, I knew what playing basketball in the state of Kentucky was all about. One of the things that I find really interesting is why players outside the state choose UK over schools in their home state. I really enjoyed reading about Mike's recruitment by Coach Joe B. Hall and how he didn't meet Coach Rupp until after he made the decision to come to Kentucky! Thanks so much, Mike and Tom, for sharing so many great stories!"—Jack "Goose" Givens, former UK basketball star and UK Hall of Famer

"Tom Leach and Mike Pratt are as good with their book as they are on the air. Their year-by-year summary of each UK basketball team since they began as a team in 2002 is not only entertaining but brings back great memories as well. A must-read for all UK basketball fans."—Jim Host, coauthor of *Changing the Game*

"*Kentucky Basketball: Two Decades Behind the Scenes* is a time capsule for Big Blue Nation. From Rupp to Calipari and everyone of note in between, Mike and Tom take you on a VIP tour through Kentucky hoops. Their experience and access give you an inside look at the inner workings of the best program in college basketball. For the last 20 years, Tom Leach and Mike Pratt have formed the best broadcasting tandem in SEC basketball. Today they transition into the best storytellers in the game. One grew up a UK fan. One wore the uniform. Their insight into and experiences with the greatest program in college basketball history will make you feel like you were courtside with them through it all."—Tom Hart, ESPN and SEC Network

"*Kentucky Basketball* is a wonderful remembrance of the wildly successful UK program over almost two decades with the men who chronicled every basket and heart-pounding moment on the air. It's as if we are eavesdropping on a conversation with Mike and Tom and getting the inside view about what truly mattered. And they would know! This book will give every Wildcat fan unique insight into one of the most distinguished programs in the college game from two of the most respected broadcasters in the business."—Kevin Harlan, CBS

KENTUCKY BASKETBALL

KENTUCKY BASKETBALL

Two Decades Behind the Scenes

MIKE PRATT AND TOM LEACH

CONTENTS

Photos follow page 78

FOREWORD

RALPH HACKER

THERE IS SOMETHING to be said about a good partner: Roy & Dale, Cisco & Pancho, Porter & Dolly, George & Tammy, Adolph & Harry. Well, you get the idea. For twenty years I had the honor of being a partner to Cawood Ledford. Now, another twenty years later, we have Tom & Mike.

I answered the phone many years ago, and on the other end was former UK basketball player—now a lawyer, and always a friend—Jim LeMaster. He simply said, "When you have the opportunity I would like you to talk to a young man, and if you believe he has potential, give him a job when you can." What a lucky break for me. That young man was Tom Leach. At that point we had no openings for another sports guy at WVLK. We already had three. But we did have an opening for a news reporter. Fortunately, Tom accepted that job after being promised that if anything opened in the sports area, he would be considered. Not only did he do a commendable job as a reporter, but he eventually became the news director. When a position opened in the sports department, he took on those responsibilities as well, doing play-by-play of high school and area colleges, hosting talk shows, and covering the University of Kentucky as a beat reporter. He did it all while also building a wonderful portfolio of the written word with his newspaper columns. One of my enduring memories of Tom occurred on Bourbon Street as he hosted his nightly talk show on a new invention, The Cell Phone This he did while engineer Tom Devine and I searched out Ralph & Kacoo's Restaurant, and he never missed a beat. To say he is talented is an understatement. To say he has earned and deserves what he has achieved is as well.

Mike Pratt was an All-American basketball player at UK. In fact, he has always been part of a team. Who does not think of Dan Issell each time Mike Pratt's name is mentioned? Even at the professional level, they were drafted onto the same team, the Kentucky Colonels. Mike went on to play, then into coaching, and finally into broadcasting. It is hard to remember when college basketball was not a 24-hour, seven-day-a-week TV event, but it used to be harder to catch a televised game, and Mike had a hand in changing that.

The Ohio Valley Conference (OVC) was looking for exposure and could not find an outlet, until a meeting with Jim Delaney, then OVC Commissioner; Ralph W. Gabbard, vice president of WKYT TV and one of the partners in the Host Communications Sports Ventures; and myself, acting as vice president of WVLK Radio. Somewhere along the way Gabbard said, "ESPN is dying for events. Why not cut a deal with them?" Delaney went to Bristol, Connecticut, and made the deal. However, it was not prime time—at least not on the East Coast—but midnight, which made it prime time on the West Coast. He then hired me, and Mike Pratt was chosen for color commentary. The very first game was on New Year's Eve at Murray State University, which is in the central time zone. At midnight eastern time the TV cameras cut to Mike and me, and there we were in our pajamas and house slippers with horns, champagne glasses, and all the New Year's confetti they could find, welcoming the ESPN national audience to a new year.

This was the first time a game had started after 9 pm on national TV, which is now commonplace.

When I left the UK broadcast team after nearly three decades, I felt strongly that Tom Leach should be the man to get the job. After all, he had assumed my football role after I hung up the reins. On behalf of Kentucky fans, I thank Jim Host for agreeing that my instincts were right. Soon after, Jim called and asked, "What do you think about Mike Pratt as the color guy for Tom?" Again, Jim was right on the money.

They may not make the money of Dick Vitale, or Keith Jackson and Frank Broyles, or Tom Hammond and Larry Conley, but in Kentucky they are loved like no others.

Whether Mike and Tom go on to another twenty years of covering the Cats, who knows? When asked why he retired at 39 years, Cawood Ledford's simple reply was, "Coach Rupp coached for 40 years. No one should be at Kentucky longer than him." They are now halfway there.

Whoever said, "Nice guys finish last," never met Tom Leach and Mike Pratt.

PREFACE

IT WAS THE summer of 2020 when Mike Pratt called with a great idea—given that we were coming up on 20 years as a broadcast team, we ought to do a book, especially since the '20 basketball season had ended in such a strange fashion because of the pandemic. Since Mike lives in Louisville and I live in Lexington, we split the difference for a planning session and had lunch at Cattlemen's Roadhouse in Frankfort to get the ball rolling. Mike and I are both big fans of TheAthletic.com, and our friend Kyle Tucker did some good work on oral history-type articles, so we took that approach. I wrote the book in a manner that hopefully puts the reader in the room with us as we discussed each season's high and low points. Mike and I would periodically tape chats on our memories of each season, starting with 2001-2002, and over the course of a few months we completed that part of the project; my wife, Robyn, then handled the transcription. From there, the book started to take shape.

The result is the kinds of conversations Mike and I (sometimes joined by our producer/engineer Jim Barnhart) would regularly have during the season (during football, too, as Mike is a big football fan and frequently calls on Sundays to rehash the previous day's game). Cawood Ledford once jokingly told me, "You sound better when they win," and it's so true, but this book takes UK fans through the ups and the downs of the two decades of Kentucky basketball since Mike and I were fortunate enough to be chosen to follow Ralph Hacker and Sam Bowie at the broadcast table. After going through each season, I also enjoyed hearing Mike tell the story of how he ended up becoming a Kentucky Wildcat, and then we had some fun putting together lists on a few fun topics.

I have been fortunate in my play-by-play role at UK to have worked with broadcasters (Mike, Jeff Van Note, Jeff Piecoro, and Dick Gabriel) who take the work on the games very seriously, but who also know how to have fun and not take *themselves* too seriously. Being a part of "teams" like that makes the job so much more enjoyable. We are so grateful for the passion of the Big Blue Nation because you never have to wonder if there's anyone out there listening. Mike and I hope all those fans enjoy joining us on this look back at the past 20 years.

—*Tom Leach*

PRATT'S PATH TO UK

LEACH: Tell me about the path that brought you to the University of Kentucky.

PRATT: We had some really good players in the city of Dayton, players that went on to play at UD, UC, and Big Ten schools. Bill Hosket played at OSU and won an Olympic gold medal in 1968. Don May was an All-American at UD and played in the NBA. We had major leaguers and we had guys that played football at Ohio State. From 1960 to '66, Dayton had three state championship teams, and two of them eliminated my school [Meadowdale] from the state tournament. It was a terrific sports town, so I got seen by playing against those [good teams].

LEACH: You played high school ball with and against some big names, too.

PRATT: [LA Dodgers catcher] Steve Yeager was at my high school, and we played baseball, football, and basketball together. Then [future baseball Hall of Famer Mike] Schmidt was at the next high school over from mine. Bob McCowan, who later followed me to Kentucky, played there, too

LEACH: How did the recruitment by UK go?

PRATT: Neil Reed, one of Adolph's recruiters, was the first guy to make contact with me early in my high school career. I had most of the Big Ten schools around me tried to recruit me. Ohio State was on me earlier and then came back hard late [in the process]. Duke tried too, and Chuck Daly was the assistant there who recruited me. But I grew up as a Dayton Flyers fan. Coach Don

Donoher, the head coach, personally recruited me. Wonderful man. I had made up mind I wasn't going far away because I wanted my family to be able to drive and see me play. But Joe Hall got back on me as a junior. I had gotten injured playing football, and he came back to see me play in December. He joked that I was fat and out of shape, but I hadn't played in several months. It got down to me wanting to leave home [but not go too far]. I could've gone to Dayton and been very happy—and they were my second choice. That was one of the hardest things I had to do was call Coach Donoher. But Rupp's Runts were so impressive. That was an attraction.

LEACH: So the Runts had a big effect on swinging you to the UK side?

PRATT: Yes. In a day when teams didn't get that national media attention, Joe would send me articles from newspapers or magazines. I fell in love with their style of play. My dad, my brother, and I drove down to see them play, and there are a lot of Kentucky fans in Dayton so they got a lot of publicity in Dayton. The only thing I had known about Kentucky when I was growing up was Cotton Nash. He was on the cover of some magazines and he was a guy I associated with Kentucky. It was cool to meet him after I got there, really nice guy. And Joe tells a story on me that I need to share with you. Joe said he had one scholarship left and there were three guys in the running for it. I was cocky and I looked Joe in the eye and said, "If you really want me, you'll save one for me." Joe likes to tell that story.

LEACH: When did you meet Coach Rupp?

PRATT: The first time I met Adolph was after my senior season [when I visited Kentucky on a recruiting trip]. I was there [at UK] for an all-star game, and I got five minutes with the Baron. He had called me a couple of times during the season when I set a scoring record in Dayton, and I had never heard anybody with that type of twang he had. He never saw me play, never saw Dan Issel play. He saw Mike Casey because he always went to the state tournament. Joe B. was the guy. He was recruiting Rick Mount and a couple of other guys, and he'd come through Dayton. Joe did all the recruiting in his car. Joe was great at selling your family.

LEACH: What do you remember about playing for Coach Rupp?

PRATT: I remember how organized he was. He was all about passing and practicing hard. He was a tough guy to play for. Back in those days, they tried to intimidate you, to see how tough you were. Harry Lancaster was brutal. He would challenge you and see how you would respond to that. I saw a lot of really good players leave because of that. Harry was also the freshman [team] coach. Adolph was kinda the good cop and Harry was the bad cop. You had to earn his respect—and keep it. I think what helped me the most was playing all three sports in high school, and my coaches challenged me. My dad did too. He climbed telephone poles and he was a tough guy. All that helped me get through it. But by the time you got to be a junior or senior and you were playing well, they backed off and dialed it down. But for a long time, my teammates thought my name was "God damn Pratt," but they could say anything to me if they just let me play.

LEACH: Your teams won three SEC championships and that was at a time when the league had players like Pistol Pete Maravich at LSU, Neal Walk at Florida, Perry Wallace at Vanderbilt. But you had two tough beats in the NCAA Tournament: the buzzer-beater in '68 that you mentioned earlier and then a 106-100 loss to Artis Gilmore's Jacksonville team in the Mideast Regional final in your final game.

PRATT: That regional had four teams ranked in the top 10 [UK, Jacksonville, Iowa, and Notre Dame]. Jacksonville played mostly a 2-3 zone even though they had one of the best goalkeepers in Gilmore. It was in the pros when I saw how athletic he was that I

3

really had a full appreciation for Artis. We had some great wins, and the league was really tough with several pros, but if you ask anybody, they will remember the losses to Ohio State and to Jacksonville. Issel fouled out with 10 minutes to go, then I fouled out and then Larry Steele. We had a great group of sophomores on that team, and they almost pulled it out. We were the highest-ranked team in that regional, and I can remember sitting on that bench when it was over with a towel over my head. And then we go in the locker room and I was sitting there and I hear this voice that was familiar. I looked up and it was Woody Hayes [legendary Ohio State football coach] consoling Adolph. I'll never forget that.

Pratt, at six four and 217 pounds, was an All-American and two-time All-SEC at UK while playing power forward. He still ranks 26th on the all-time scoring list and 22nd in rebounding. He was an Academic All-American too. Pratt is a member of the UK Athletics Hall of Fame, the state of Kentucky Athletic Hall of Fame, and the Ohio Basketball Hall of Fame. After a stint with the Kentucky Colonels of the ABA, Pratt entered the coaching ranks. He was an assistant to Lee Rose on UNCC's 1977 Final Four team and later became the head coach at Charlotte.

THE BROADCAST TEAM

LEACH: Having done UK football games since 1997, I was certainly hopeful to add the basketball duties whenever Ralph Hacker decided to step aside. In the summer of 2001, after selling his group of radio stations the year before, Ralph was ready to retire and Jim Host called with the offer to do Kentucky basketball. I'll always remember that moment, having dreamed of sitting in Cawood Ledford's seat when I was growing up listening to the Wildcats' games on radio. But joining the UK Radio Network was not really something on your radar at that time, was it?

PRATT: No, it wasn't. I don't think we'd ever met, but I listened to you and my good buddy Jeff Van Note on football. I was talking with my guys at Fox Sports South about renewing my TV contract and I get a call from "Brooksie," Brooks Downing [sports information director at UK at the time], and he tells me Sam Bowie is retiring and "we want to know if you'd be interested in the job," and I said, "Let me think about it." I was gone every weekend for about 12 weeks with Fox, and my wife was happy with the thought I'd been around more often—to do more chores [*chuckles*]. I got to thinking about this and called Brooksie back and he said, "Host will call you." I called my daughter for her advice—a broadcast journalism major at Missouri—and her great line was "Dad, you're not getting any younger, and TV is former younger people."

Radio jobs like this don't pay as well as TV work, so Mike knew he would make less per game than he was getting at Fox, but the initial offer was less than he needed to make the change.

PRATT: [Athletics director] Larry Ivy and Brooks called me and said, "We're gonna get this thing done," so we found a meeting spot on the money. I told Jim, "Let's just go year to year and see how it goes." I had always done television, but radio is different, as you know. I wouldn't have left that Fox gig for anybody else but UK. Jim said, "Why don't you get with Tom and do a tape to get a feel for each other?" and we met in his office and did half a game, and that was enough for me. I knew we could hit it off and grow this thing. It's really been fun. Brings back a lot of memories, like I'll slip down to Alligator Alley when we're playing at Florida. We have a great team. Jimmy Barnhart is the best producer in the world, and I think the three of us fit well. It's like a family. It's been wonderful.

LEACH: I remember my initial thought was that working with you reminded me of working with "Noter" [Jeff Van Note] and Piecoro. Both were always well prepared and very professional and took the job very seriously—but not themselves. Guys like Host and Hacker didn't care much for high-maintenance people working for them, and that's the kind of team we've always had.

PRATT: Sam [Bowie, Pratt's predecessor in the analyst role] couldn't have been nicer. He wished me well. He said his first year they won a championship [in 1998], and he hoped it would be the same for me. "Mace" [Kyle Macy], who had done it before, couldn't have been nicer either. I knew coming in that television was the analyst's show and I knew radio was the play-by-play guy's show, so I needed to know how to read you. I had to figure out your rhythm and plug mine into it.

LEACH: And we had both worked with Ralph. I came to his station in 1984, and he surely had as great an influence on my career as anyone I worked for. I remembered watching you and Ralph doing the Ohio Valley Conference game of the week at midnight on Fridays one season, so I knew if Ralph liked working with you, I would as well.

PRATT: Ralph and I go so far back, to when he was breaking in the business in Richmond. We had a ball doing those games.

LEACH: This latest season [2020–2021] was certainly unusual. The only non–Rupp Arena game we saw in person was the one in the SEC Tournament. Otherwise, our producer, Jim Barnhart, would set up the equipment in a conference room at Memorial Coliseum and Greg Gorham from UK Sports Video would coordinate with the TV network to get us a feed. They did their jobs flawlessly, but there were times when we lost the signal, and I grew to appreciate fans' frustrations with ESPN dropping other things into the broadcast while the game was going on because I'm trying to call what is happening and I'm watching an interview. I was grateful we had games to work, but that was a sometimes frustrating way to have to do them.

PRATT: I like to watch the bench and I missed that. The body language, the communication, how the players respond to coaching. When we did it on TV, we only got one feed, and it was difficult to see the bench. And what's also important is what happens off the ball, and I couldn't see that. We just saw action on the ball. And I like to go to practice and watch what they do and see how the players interact. How do they react to Cal? He'll coach you hard when you do something, but he has a great knack for putting his arm around them and being positive too.

LEACH: As for our jobs in general, one of the greatest compliments we received came from Jim O'Connell, the longtime college basketball writer for the Associated Press. He was like a walking, talking Google search for college basketball because it sometimes seemed like he saw every game. I used to listen to him on Tony Kornheiser's radio show, and it was such an honor to meet him early in my tenure in this job. I was interviewing in an NCAA Tournament media room one year about Kentucky and after we finished, while the recorder was still rolling, he told me a story about a family function that he ducked out of to go watch the end of a Kentucky game. He said he found our broadcast on WHAS while driving back to his home and ended up staying in the car to listen to the end of the game rather than going inside to watch it. He complimented us on the job we did on that game, and I considered that a tremendous honor, coming from "the OC," as Kornheiser called hm. He passed a few years ago, but he's one of the memorable people you get to meet in having these jobs like you and I do.

PRATT: Jim was big-time as far as college basketball writers. I've run into a lot of people over the years that have tuned us in that you might not have expected. Marty Brennaman always listened, for example.

2002

Kentucky started the season ranked fourth in the nation, but lost its opener to Western Kentucky 64-52 at Rupp Arena, getting "outplayed in every phase of the game," according to Coach Tubby Smith. That set the tone for a frustrating season for the BBN, as some off-the-court issues led to the nickname "Team Turmoil." Still, the season produced some memorable moments, including two by Tayshaun Prince—hitting five consecutive three-pointers to start the North Carolina game and a 41-point game in the NCAA Tournament.

LEACH: Our first season as the men's basketball broadcast team went even better than I hoped from the standpoint of on-air chemistry, but things didn't go quite as smoothly for the Wildcats. Starting center Jason Parker was lost for the season to a knee injury suffered at Big Blue Madness in October. Western Kentucky upset fourth-ranked Kentucky in the opening game, and there were several disciplinary issues that cropped up over the course of a campaign that led to the squad getting hung with the nickname "Team Turmoil." But Tayshaun Prince provided two signature performances. The first was hitting five three-pointers to start the game against North Carolina, and the other was his 41-point explosion against Tulsa in the second round of the NCAA Tournament. Ironically, it occurred in the same city [St. Louis] as the 41-point night Jack Givens produced in the 1978 national title game.

PRATT: I love the way he played. He didn't say anything to anybody. He didn't say crap; he just played. He was like a silent assassin. He cared about where he should be on the offense or the defense. Skinny guy, rail thin, but man, he understood the game. Tayshaun was one of my favorite players because of the fact that he knew how to play, and he didn't waste time barking.

LEACH: Tayshaun reminded me of a player, Gayle Sayers, in the NFL, who was my first favorite player as a kid. Sayers made it look effortless. He glided. He was obviously fast, but it wasn't just the raw speed that wowed you, it was just how effortless he made everything look, and I thought Tayshaun was like that.

PRATT: And these days, they all look for the great athlete, the guy who's long and all those things athletically. Tayshaun was a good athlete, don't get me wrong, but he wasn't at the level we see guys now. But what he was¾he was smart. And I like him for all those reasons and also he was a throwback player, which is a compliment from me because I had the chance to play with a lot of really good players after Kentucky, and most of them just played the game. When I got to the Colonels and I played with all those guys like Les Hunter, Cincy Powell, Jim "Goose" Ligon, Artis Gilmore, Dan Issel, Louie Dampier. They all were really smart players. They all knew their limitations and they played to their strengths, and I think you can say that about Tayshaun. He played to his strengths.

LEACH: I always loved watching Magic and Bird the year they owned the stage in college, in '79. They both just dominated games and rarely played very high off the floor, and Tayshaun was that way. He didn't have to wow you with athleticism. He had that element to his game—just remember that famous blocked shot he had against Reggie Miller in the NBA playoffs for the Pistons—but he could dominate a game without making those kinds of plays too.

PRATT: He utilized everything he had. He played to his strengths, much like the guys you mentioned. They weren't going out of their area of expertise, and you had to stop them¾and that was really hard to do. When Tayshaun was playing to his strengths and you had to try to stop him and force him to do something he didn't want to do, that was hard. That was really hard.

LEACH: We should talk about the Carolina game when he hit the five straight threes. That's a moment I still hear about from fans from time to time. I remember two things about it—number one is just how loud it was as he hit one after another. And the other thing was when he had hit four in a row, and I think it was Gerald Fitch came up with a steal or a loose ball and threw it ahead to Tayshaun, and it was just so fun to see a guy in a groove because he just stopped about one step past the midcourt circle and launched it. You could just kind of see it in Tayshuan's eyes that it didn't matter where he shot it from, it was going to go in.

PRATT: He was in the zone in that game [finishing with 31 points]. We all realize as players: you get into that zone where everything around you is tuned out. You are all by yourself playing a game, shooting on the playground, and there's no pressure. There isn't anything but you, the ball, and the game. He didn't worry about anything. He just got to where he wanted to go and shot the ball.

LEACH: Tayshaun really understood how to score too.

PRATT: Oh, yeah. He knew how to create. He was a creator off the bounce, and he knew where to go to get his shot and how to get it. High basketball IQ. And he got the foul line a lot too.

LEACH: While Tayshaun provided the most memorable moments from that season, there were some odd ones too. The first one that comes to mind was Rashaad Carruth's unspoken protest. He came in highly touted, McDonald's All-American, but had not played much on a team that had quite a few veterans on it, so when the Cats hosted Kentucky State on December 15, he played some but refused to take a shot. Then, the next game, against number one-ranked Duke at the Meadowlands [in the Jimmy V Classic], he had the best game he would have as a Wildcat. We finally saw that jumper we had heard about, and he led them in scoring with 19 points. Unfortunately, Jay Williams, now famous as an ESPN announcer, had one of those nights that great players sometimes have, and he went for 38, and Duke came back to win a great game in OT. They rebounded with three straight wins, but they dropped the league opener at Mississippi State in overtime after leading by 16 at the half. And I also remember an unusual postgame interview you had with Cliff Hawkins at South Carolina. He hit the game-winner in a 51-50 victory, and yet I remember his facial expression when he was talking with you on our postgame show was like a man who had just lost his dog.

PRATT: He was stone-faced. I think I said to him, "Man, that was a special shot. That was a shot heard from one end of Kentucky to the other," and he just looked at me with a blank stare. I thought he would have been smiling from ear to ear.

LEACH: That season got off to a bad start when an unranked Western Kentucky came in for the opener and upset the Cats at Rupp by 12. It seemed to be an up-and-down season from there, and when they got upset in their first game at the SEC Tournament, I think everybody thought the season was over. As it turned out, they rallied to play pretty well in their three NCAA Tournament games, beating Valparaiso and Tulsa before losing to eventual national champion Maryland. I thought it was a tribute to Coach Tubby Smith that they bounced back the way they did.

PRATT: Absolutely. They really heard Tubby, they reacted. I mean, you've got quality people here with Tayshaun Prince and Keith Bogans—quality guys. I think they understood the game, but they also had an idea of the big picture, and they listened to Tubby.

LEACH: What do you think got off the rails in that season? Because they came back so strong the next year.

PRATT: You know, I think maybe it was just the combination of players. As you've heard me say many times, pieces don't fit, and I'm not so sure the pieces fit on that team as far as attitude. And that's big. I think that when you start a season with high expectations, which Kentucky always does, and you lose your opener, it takes the air out of a lot of things for us. Getting beat by 12 at home was a killer way to get started. And that injury to Parker in the preseason was big. When all of that stuff happens, either off the floor or on the floor, I think it does shake you up as a team.

LEACH: As we would later see with Cal in this past season, it's a different kind of challenge as a coach when a season gets off the rails at a place like Kentucky. And you better have a strong will and a lot of self-confidence to coach your way through those times. From your coaching perspective, what did you see in how Tubby handled that season?

PRATT: He really communicated with his players. They all seemed to understand and really like Tubby. I think he did better in that regard than maybe communicating with the public, with the fan base. He was good with the fan base, don't get me wrong, but I think the Tub man was really, really good at communicating with his players. Consequently, his calling card was defense and rebounding. That's the hardest thing to really get young players to do. People complained about his offense, but they played the heck outta D and rebounded, and I think that goes back to how he was able to communicate with his players. I thought he was always in control. If he got angry, he didn't lose track of the game. He made really good adjustments, and at halftime is where he was at his best.

LEACH: This was the season when Rick Pitino made his return to Rupp, but as the coach of Kentucky's archrival, and Kentucky won big. I remembered being happy for Tubby that the game went so well because it's tough if the guy or lady that you replace comes in and beats you. A few years later, after another loss in Lexington, he would say, "I coached eight years here and I loved my teams. I expect to be booed. It doesn't bother me because it's a compliment," but I don't believe that he believed that. In a rivalry situation, I don't think it's realistic to switch sides and yet expect you'll still be beloved by the fans of the school you left. Kentucky fans should always be grateful for what Pitino did for the UK program, but I also understand why they could not show that appreciation when he was coaching at the rival program. However, at some point in the future, I think he will have the much more pleasant return experience at Rupp Arena that he deserves.

PRATT: I didn't understand the depth of the animosity toward him. Not that I'm a friend of Rick or anything, but he had a lot of success at UK. That surprised me. Tubby low-keyed it, if I remember right, but the fans were on Rick's buns. Tubby is all class and he took it on himself to try and make it easier for his former boss. Tubby is a coach's coach. He believes in coaches and believes in those relationships. He might fight and fuss with them about some things, but bottom line: he is a coach's coach. I remember him doing that because of all the buildup about that game. The fans still haven't forgiven Rick for leaving. The Big Blue Nation loves their team and their coaches, and they felt like they were dumped on. I remember the electricity in that place was amazing. It was one of those games where you could cut the electricity in the air with a knife.

2003

The concept of halftime adjustments is often an overrated aspect of a game. Coaches will tell you that it's not so much a change in strategy or personnel as it is getting players refocused on the game plan or perhaps calling a play or two to try to get a player back on track in a given game. In the 2003 season, a game at Vanderbilt marked one of those most dramatic reversals of form from one half of basketball to another—and it keyed one of the most impressive streaks in UK basketball history. The Wildcats were down by eight points at the break but came out with a suffocating defensive effort that produced a 74-52 victory. The next nine victories all came by double-digit margins, including a rout of top-ranked Florida—the best part of a streak of 26 wins in a row. It was Tubby Smith's best shot at a second national title, but an ankle injury to Keith Bogans in a Sweet 16 win over Wisconsin preceded an upset loss to Marquette in the regional final in Minneapolis. Oh, what might have been with a healthy Bogans!

PRATT: You're playing to get to the Final Four, and for Marquette it had been how long since Al McGuire won the title? [1977] There was a lot of juice on their side. Add to that, they knew Bogans was hobbled. Everybody talked about it before the game. Is he gonna be healthy; is he not? Is he gonna play; is he not? So they get out there, they see him warming up. They're probably taking a peek— you know the coaches are. Then when you see him at the tip, how he's not moving the same way he once did, not only are you pumped to go to the Final Four, now it's blood in the water and you go after 'em. I know the UK coaches were very concerned about Bogans' ability to play in the Elite Eight game. They had his ankle wrapped up pretty doggone tight. They were very concerned about his ability to perform at his level—not just play, but they needed him as the real Keith Bogans, and they didn't really think that was possible. Keith tried, and you gotta give the kid a lot of credit. He was a tough, hardnosed basketball player. He's not gonna stop Dwayne Wade, but you could slow him down, and Keith had the tools to do that, the physical tools, to slow him down. Not shut him down but slow him down. You might get into a standoff.

LEACH: Marquette's Dwayne Wade was one of the country's top players, but he chose this day to give us a preview of the future NBA Hall of Famer he would become. His triple-double was incredible, but I have to think healthy Bogans would have given Kentucky a better matchup there. After a barrage of first-half threes put them in a 19-point hole at the half, Kentucky made a bit of a run, but it was just too much to overcome. It's a shame because that team had everything it needed to win it all.

PRATT: Wade was able to score at will, in the paint, around the basket, he got a couple putbacks. He was possessed, and Keith couldn't do anything. They had him in almost a cast on that ankle, and he had no shot. That's the interesting thing about guys—now, maybe and guys then—they could smell blood in the water, man. Wade could smell blood in the water. He knew Keith was hobbled. That was a terrific performance. Kansas ended up winning it, and we would have played Kansas in the first game and I think this team was built to win it all. If you look at the lineup, they could score inside, they could score off the bounce, they had enough perimeter shooting to keep you honest. It was a typical Tubby team. They could knock your buns down in a heartbeat. Yeah. I think that's the best team he had.

LEACH: Kentucky nearly got Pittsburgh in that Elite Eight game. Marquette was life-and-death to beat Pitt with a really good player from Lexington—Jaron Brown. And Kentucky had all it wanted with Wisconsin, for that matter, in that semifinal game. The crowd was with the Badgers, but they ultimately had no answer for Marquis Estill. He had one of his best games [28 points on 12/18 shooting], and Bo Ryan was never going to play zone to try to get some help on him.

PRATT: So we get Marquette. We match up pretty good. Then 'Quis opens his mouth about the center from Marquette who had transferred from Mississippi State [Robert Jackson, who Estill said he didn't remember playing against]. That was on the billboard, we found out afterward. Tubby said something to me in between games when our paths crossed. He said, "What was he thinking?" At that point in the NCAA, there's a gazillion writers from all over and they'll pick up on anything and that day [against Kentucky], Jackson had a really good first half. Really good. After the game he said comments by Marquis motivated him, and then with Bogans' hurt coming out of that Wisconsin game, it became a tough matchup and Wade was all world that afternoon. [Marquette won 83-69. Wade's line was 29-11-11, while Jackson had a career day with 24 points and 15 rebounds].

LEACH: There are a few other memorable moments from that season that we should discuss. First, let's go back to the annual Indiana game, played at Freedom Hall. That was a good IU team that had won the Maui tournament in which Kentucky finished third earlier in the season. There was a play late where Coach Mike Davis thought their best player, Bracey Wright, had been fouled, and he storms out to the free-throw line. He immediately gets T'd up, and then referee Bert Smith showed amazing patience. As an official, I'm sure you would rather not toss a coach out of a close game like that, and Bert walked from the baseline to where we were seated at midcourt, just repeating, "Walk away." Coach Davis couldn't do it, and Bert ultimately had to call the second technical and Kentucky won the game 70-64.

Let's also talk about the big win down at North Carolina a

little before that [98-81]. The thing I remember there is that Erik Daniels hadn't been playing, and he came in and showed a spark and then eventually grew into a starting role for that team. He's one of those players that started out as a guard earlier in his basketball, had a growth spurt, and then he had those guard skills in a much taller body.

PRATT: He knew how to play. He wasn't gonna step out on the floor and shoot threes or anything, but boy, he could rebound and figure out a way with his body to score. He was a fun kid to watch. Left-handed.

LEACH: The other game that stands out for me from that season was the rout of Florida. They had just moved to the number one spot in the polls on Monday, and then they come to Rupp for a Tuesday night game. Each season, there is always a game or two or three where the atmosphere is just on another level—and you can sense it when you walk into the arena. I always remember feeling that "buzz" in the air that night when I arrived two hours before tip-off.

PRATT: The Florida and Kentucky rivalry really had become something special. The electricity gets like that for certain games. As a player, I sensed it the minute you walk through the tunnel at the old Coliseum. You sensed it. You might even sense it when you came for the game and saw all of the students out there. As broadcasters we get there early and we feel it. It reminds me back in my day, of when Tennessee would come in or Vandy, who was really good. Or "Pistol" [Pete Maravich at LSU]. We had some nonconference games that were good but boy, those other games, they were electric.

LEACH: That night was that team at its best. Their defense just overwhelmed the Gators [17/50 from the field, 19 turnovers by a number one team] and on offense, when I look back at that box score, what jumps out is 19 assists on 30 baskets for the Cats.

PRATT: Somewhere in January they figured out the combination of inside and out and they really played well with it. 'Quis would give it up and he could power move inside. They really spun the ball on the outside to find an open shooter. They had worked that out. But it was their defense that really bothered people. I mean, that defense was pretty damn good. They had shot blockers, they had guys who could pressure out. Gerald Fitch was a helluva on-ball defender and so was Bogans. You had two guys pushing out front defensively, in your face and able to do things and keep people out of the paint. Then you had 'Quis back there and Daniels. They could block shots. Chuck Hayes. He could guard five positions. What a plus he was. He was really good at giving help too. He was so smart. He saw things break down and he'd move over and take a charge. He got a lot of off-ball rebounds on the off side.

LEACH: That was maybe the perfect Tubby team for his style.

PRATT: Absolutely.

2004

The 2004 team surely outperformed expectations to finish 27-5, win the East and then the SEC Tournament, and with some losses by other clubs around the country on Selection Sunday weekend, the Wildcats ended up going into the NCAA Tournament as the number one overall seed. That team had drawn the ire of Wildcat fans with a disappointing nine-point home loss to Louisville on the Saturday after Christmas but by March, Big Blue Nation seemed convinced that this team was going to get the title that the Cats had missed out on capturing the year before.

PRATT: They had to play a little different that year [because of the losses of Bogans outside and Estill inside]. You had Fitch and Daniels, Kelenna Azubuike, Hayes, and Cliff Hawkins. That's a small team. Kelenna was the best athlete on the team. Fitch was the best shooter or scorer. And Hawkins ran the team well. They had five guys in double figures. They went out to the Wooden Classic and beat UCLA, beat Michigan State, and blew out Indiana [80-41 at the RCA Dome in Indianapolis].

LEACH: That Michigan State game was the only basketball game I've ever needed binoculars to call. Good thing I had not removed them from my backpack after football season. They called it the "Basket Bowl" at Ford Field in Detroit, and it was a test run for changing the configuration of seats at Final Fours: putting the court in the middle of what would be the football field at an NFL game and then selling out all the seats. By the time they used this for Final Fours, they used inclined seating for better sightlines, but for this thing, it looked like the biggest wedding you'd ever see. There was an elevated court and then hundreds of white, wooden folding chairs on the turf so unless you were on the front row or so, you didn't have much of a view. And then we were working from the football press box so I've always said Hawkins at six foot one looked to be the same size as seven foot three Shagari Alleyne. That's why I needed the binoculars. It was either that or call the game off the big scoreboard monitor, and I wasn't sure about the delay on that signal versus the live action. As for the game—wow, were they sharp that day: 60 percent shooting, Fitch had 25, and it was a glimpse of that team at its best. And Chuck Hayes was really good [17 points, 12 rebounds]. Rebounding is also big when you play Michigan State, and Kentucky outrebounded the Spartans that day.

PRATT: You know Chuck Hayes never averaged more than 10.9 a game, but there might not have been a guy during those 10 years [in which Tubby coached] that influenced the outcome of the game more than Chuck. He would board, he would defend, he could guard five positions. He was always around the ball at the defensive end. For a guy who's six five at the most, he influenced the game. He didn't have to have the ball but he could influence the game as good as anybody during that 10-year stretch of games.

LEACH: Tubby told me one time in a pregame show that people didn't realize how Chuck covered up for other mistakes. I equate it to a great center fielder. Chuck was always in the right place, and something Dwane Casey told me about Chuck was that he "understood angles"—again like that great outfielder or shortstop who uses a keen understanding of the game to always put himself or herself in the right spot. He understood the game so well, that's probably why he stayed in the league as long as he did.

PRATT: 10 years later, along came the Grant Williams kid at Tennessee. He was a Chuck-type player. He is with Boston. Coaches love that type of guy. The way teams were constructed then, everybody can't have the ball—other guys have to do other things and be happy. From what I read and what I saw, even in the pros,

Chuck was happy with not being the ball-dominant guy. He played hard and rebounded and did the little things off the bench. That kinda attitude, man, is missing with a lot of guys over the last few years. Not just at Kentucky but across the board in basketball.

LEACH: The Grant Williams comparison is a good one. I know fans got frustrated with his "flops" and I get that, but I enjoyed watching both him and Admiral Schofield. Loved how hard they competed and how much they seemed to enjoy playing the game. But back to Chuck, I really thought either he or Erik was going to get a triple-double that year because both of them were such good passers. I don't know that you and I saw two guys play off each other better than those did with their passing in and around the lane area. Two very high basketball IQ guys who made their teammates better.

PRATT: They were both so unselfish. Erik could really score. He was six eight and he was really good at angles. He could draw a crowd and finish, and then Chuck was the beneficiary of when the defense left. Erik understood it and could get it to Chuck and Chuck just caught it and scored. And Chuck could sucker that defense in and flip it over to Erik. They complemented each other very well.

LEACH: All of those guys on that team understood their roles and how to play. I think that's why they were so good in close games. They won a one-pointer at Mississippi State when Daniels picked up a deflected pass off an inbounds play with a second or two left—he was in the right place at the right time, and that's not always just luck. They won a one-pointer in OT at Tennessee when Cliff elevated from the Tennessee logo [probably 30 feet out] and drained a three-pointer. They were unbeaten in one-possession games [5-0] until that last loss in the NCAA Tournament to UAB.

PRATT: That UAB game, they threw up a zone and outside of Fitch, we didn't have consistent outside shooting. Kelenna wasn't there yet and Chuck and Hawkins were off and on. UAB had a nice ball club. They were small like us. Relatively speaking. That was a helluva game, a buzzer game.

LEACH: UAB made eight threes, they forced UK into 16 turnovers, and the 18 offensive rebounds were big because they neutralized some good first-shot defensive possessions for Kentucky. Being down nine at halftime to a much lower seed might have caused that team to play a little tight too, because those guys had been denied a Final Four they thought they were going to get the year before. And I remember a very questionable late charging call on Azubuike that was big. Still, they had a shot in the air late by Fitch that would have likely won the game. It seemed like the same play that Tubby ran for a big late bucket to beat North Carolina back in December. Fitch got a good look this time too, but nobody makes 'em all. I can't imagine anyone else I would rather have had take that shot at that time.

PRATT: He was one of my favorites. He would just compete at both ends and he was not afraid to take a big shot. Gerald might have been the toughest guy on the team. Either him or Chuck. But Gerald wore his toughness on his sleeve. You knew when he was focused in just by watching him and his body language. When he got that look, he was dangerous. He was a good rebounder too. He understood the game and where the rebounds were going to come. Tubby loved him—how could you not? Calipari would love to have a guy like that [in this 2021 season]. He and Erik and Chuck had a toughness to them, and maybe that's why that team was so damn good.

LEACH: Some media members made a big deal of Nolan Richardson, the former Arkansas coach, helping his protégé UAB coach Mike Anderson in preparing for Kentucky. Did you think that was a significant angle to the game?

PRATT: No, I didn't make much of that. I think it was just chatter. Mike Anderson knew what Tubby's team wanted to do and vice versa.

2005

As you can tell by now, Mike and I were big fans of Chuck Hayes. There was probably no player for whom we rooted harder to get to a Final Four. As a freshman, in a season that went a little off the rails at times, Hayes became the go-to guy for the media folks covering the team because of his composure through some difficult times. Then, in the next two years, he was a key player on two Final Four–caliber teams that lost in upsets. Chuck was all about winning, and in 2005, his competitive fire nearly lifted his team to a goal that was in reality more of a long shot than it was for the other teams on which he played.

LEACH: Whereas those previous two teams were a great fit for their coach, this one was an atypical Tubby team in that it was much more reliant on newcomers. Patrick Sparks had transferred in from Western Kentucky and you had what was Tubby's highest-rated recruiting class with Randolph Morris, Joe Crawford, Rajon Rondo, and Ramel Bradley, but Tubby was always at his best with a veteran group that fully understood ball-line defense and that had been battle-tested, and this team featured what was probably too many newcomers.

PRATT: Tubby liked a more experienced team where he was able to get his offense and defense down with the guys. I think he was in his groove as a coach with developing players. One of the complaints about Tubby was that he didn't recruit the five-star guys, and Kentucky fans are wrapped up in the recruiting rankings, as are many fan bases. He got guys he thought he could win with and guys he could mold. That influx of new players—it took them awhile to learn what he wanted.

LEACH: I thought you really saw some of that team's flaws when they lost by 13 at North Carolina in early December. That was Roy's first national title team at Carolina and the Tar Heels beat Kentucky up to the tune of 51-30 on the boards that day. That's a stat you rarely saw for one of Tubby's teams. But one of the high points of that season came a couple of weeks later when they beat U of L at Freedom Hall 60-58 on those Sparks free throws. Kentucky was 32-16 at halftime, and then Patrick Sparks took over in the second half. He finished with 25 points and when he got fouled late with Kentucky down one, I had no doubt he was going to make those free throws. [That comeback tied with 1994's Mardi Gras Miracle at LSU for the largest halftime deficit overcome in UK history.]

PRATT: Sparks was clutch, man, he was clutch. He had a quick release, being smallish, at the guard spot. He knew how to get open and that ball was gone, man. The only thing that bothered him were taller players. And he could really work his magic without the ball.

LEACH: Sparks found his way back into that zone down at Alabama in February. He made seven threes and that's one of my favorite things to watch in basketball, when a good shooter has that look in his eye that he can't miss. That was probably the highlight of the league season, which ended with a one-point loss at Florida, and when the Gators dominated Kentucky in the rematch a week later in the SEC Tournament, I think most fans wrote off that team as a Final Four contender. But they got it back on track. They caught a break in getting Utah, which had upset the three-seed [Oklahoma], and then I think there was a consensus that they caught another one when Michigan State upset the region's top seed, Duke, in the first half of that Sweet 16 doubleheader. I remember you and I sitting at courtside watching that game and you saying anybody thinking that way might be mistaken because Michigan State looked like a team on a roll.

PRATT: You and I always go over for the public shootarounds, and that was the first time I had seen Duke in person, and I thought, "We want to play Duke," and then I watched Michigan State and thought, "These guys are a lot like us." I knew Michigan State was going to be a handful. They were a lot like us.

LEACH: Those games in the Sweet 16 set the stage for an epic battle on Sunday afternoon. With a better twist of fate, Sean Woods in '92 and Sparks that year would have had shots featured for years to come on those CBS highlight reels. When Sparks hit that shot at the end of regulation, we couldn't go to a scheduled commercial break because you didn't want to be away from the game when a ruling was made on whether Sparks's shot was a game-tying three- or a two-pointer that would have meant a win for the Spartans. And it seemed like it took referee Jim Burr and his crew 10 or more minutes to make the ruling, and in the meantime, we had no TV monitor to watch to give us some insight on how it looked.

PRATT: It was just seconds when that ball was bounding around on the rim, but it seemed like minutes. Sparks was like Gerald Fitch in having that mentality to take big shots. He got my attention in that first game he played against Kentucky when he was a freshman at Western Kentucky. You and I had a conversation about how did we [UK] miss on him. Patrick lived for that game. Maybe he thought he should have been recruited by Kentucky, but he got my attention right then and there.

LEACH: The team that ties a game in that manner usually seems to have the edge in overtime and that happened here, until Michigan State got three offensive rebounds in succession with Kentucky up by four. I will always think the Cats would have won that game if they'd gotten one of those rebounds and unfortunately, Chuck Hayes was sitting at the scorer's table waiting to check in, having been held out of the lineup to start the OT because he had four fouls. I remember a tear running down Chuck's face as they played "My Ol' Kentucky Home" on Senior Night and I remember the pure joy on his face when he came over to talk with you after scoring the game-winner against LSU in the SEC Tourney semifinal win, and I would love to have him seen him get to celebrate going to a Final Four that day in Texas.

PRATT: No question, he was the leader. He was Tubby's kinda guy. That kid was a coach's dream: multiple position defensive player. One situation like that can define a year. One guy or two guys who are important for all-around reasons. Chuck only averaged 10.9 that season, but it wasn't about his points, it was about his rebounds, his defense. He was willing to do the dirty work.

2006

This was still a team that was short on experience for Tubby's system, which worked best with older players. Four of the top five scorers for the season were sophomores, and while the squad did not lack for talent, the chemistry never seemed quite what it needed to be. That was perhaps most evident in a 73-46 loss at Kansas on January 7, and that was followed by a 0-2 start in the SEC season. But despite what the group might have lacked in chemistry, there was no shortage of competitive fire among guys like Sparks, Rondo, Crawford, and Bradley, and that "fight" showed up big-time in the team's final game, a near-upset of top-seed UConn in the second round of the NCAA Tournament.

PRATT: If Kelenna Azubuike came back for his senior year, it might have been a different story. He went from 11 points a game as a sophomore to 14 as a junior. We all talked about how he looked like he was really confident, making plays off the bounce, using his strength, very aggressive. The conversation I had with [Assistant Coach David] Hobbs and Tubby was that they bemoaned the fact that Kelenna didn't come back. They would have had a different team and then later on in the year, a guy like him really knew his game. On that team, the only other guy who could do that might've been Joe Crawford. Kelenna really became an aggressive player. That's what they could've used that year, a go-to guy that's either gonna make a hoop or get fouled. Morris, he couldn't do it. He played well but he wasn't an aggressive player.

LEACH: Morris didn't play until January 10 because of that fax deal, where he had to sit the first part of the season when he decided he wanted to return to Kentucky after initially thinking he was heading to the pros. That was just one of several ways in which that team just never seemed to get in sync.

PRATT: Randolph Morris was kinda in and out. He averaged 13 a game. Some days he was there, some days he wasn't. Inconsistent. And here's the other thing—you got some guys who were relatively young, four sophomores, one senior. I'm not so sure they all played as hard as Tubby wanted. Most of Tubby's teams would beat you up defensively, play hard. This team was more offensive-oriented, maybe. I think they expected more out of Randolph than 13 a game. I'm sure he led in rebounds. Rondo for the most part played very hard. Really a terrific defensive player. He probably fit pretty well with Bradley because Bradley would shoot it, Sparks would shoot it, but outside of Rondo, I don't think we had guys who fit Tubby's mold defensively. Particularly you saw that when they went to Philadelphia to play the Connecticut team. They had plenty of chances to win that game. They gave up a rebound on a free throw to Boone. They were young. They didn't have the mental toughness that was needed with starting four sophomores and a senior. It wasn't a typical defensive effort by a Tubby Smith team.

LEACH: That team never seemed to get in sync. That was most clearly the case in that game at Kansas. I remember being excited about working a game from a historic venue like Allen Fieldhouse, and that game was over early and then it was followed by two straight losses to start league play. But one of the outliers in terms of performance in that season came when they beat a fourth-ranked Louisville team at Rupp Arena. Rondo basically beat them by himself, scoring 25 points, and I remember a reporter asking Pitino in the postgame about Rondo as an NBA prospect and he said Rondo would be great because you could not keep him from getting to wherever he wanted to go on the court—and he was right about that.

PRATT: Rondo clashed with Tubby from time to time. Rajon always thought he could control the game by himself, and Tubby's defense all revolved around the help side and staying connected defensively and there wasn't a whole lot of freelancing. Now Rajon was really good at that—and knew he was good at it—and that kinda grated on Tubby because he was trying to connect everybody. The kicker was that the kid typically got it right.

LEACH: I remember a game Kentucky won over South Carolina on an improbable last-second three-pointer by Rondo [he only hit 27 percent of them for the season]. I asked Tubby about that unlikely game-winning play when he came out courtside for the postgame radio show and he went "off." It was as mad as I think I ever saw him. He said something like, "You think I called that play? He did that on his own."

PRATT: I went to a fundraising event for the Tubby Smith Foundation after the game and Tubby pulled me aside and he was still livid.

LEACH: For all of the ups and downs, I give those guys credit for how they came together for that second-round game in the NCAA Tournament against UConn. UConn was the top seed, ranked second in the nation, and Kentucky nearly upset them. One thing about guys like Rondo and Sparks was that they were both fierce competitors, the kind of guys you would want on your team if you were playing pickup and had to win to stay on the court. And that day, we saw those two at their best. Sparks had 28, Rondo nearly had a triple-double, and looking back at the box score, it is worth nothing how well Bobby Perry developed over the course of the season. I had forgotten that he scored 20 in that game.

PRATT: If it wasn't for a couple of bounces that gave them extra opportunities, we could have won that thing. Sparks and Rondo played really well. They would line up and compete against anybody. And they played really well together at times.

2007

An eleven-game winning streak in the middle of this season raised hopes for a return to glory, but the optimism faded in a series of mostly close losses. From January 20 through the end of the regular season, Kentucky lost four games by five or fewer points and another that went to overtime. The final blow came in the Cats' second SEC Tournament game when Jodie Meeks was poised to close out a hard-fought win over Mississippi State but his second free throw was wiped off the books with a lane violation, leading to an overtime loss that seemed to be the knockout punch of the season for this team. Dropping seven of the final 12 games heading into the SEC Tournament had the Big Blue Nation in a very sour mood, and what turned out to be Tubby Smith's final season at the helm of the UK program slipped away quietly with a 12-point loss to Kansas. Those final two seasons for Tubby Smith coincided with Billy Donovan's best two Florida teams, as the Gators won consecutive national championships.

LEACH: I don't think anybody really thought that loss to Kansas in the second round of the NCAA Tournament was Tubby's last game at Kentucky when it happened. Were you surprised that he went to Minnesota shortly thereafter?

PRATT: I sensed that he was ready maybe to move on. It seemed to me that he just wasn't a happy camper, but I didn't think he'd go to Minnesota. But that's why you have agents. You go to your agent and you say, "Get me outta here."

LEACH: The job can wear on you. He had to follow Rick, who had a great run at a difficult time for Kentucky basketball in the early '90's. Tubby wins the title in 1998 in one of the all-time great coaching jobs, getting that team back on track in mid-February for a championship run, but he was following a legend, and whenever you are the guy or lady in that spot, I'm sure it feels like nothing you ever accomplish is enough.

PRATT: On top of that, '06 and '07, Florida wins the national championship. And I think at that point, the recruiting issue, among many people, came up for Tubby. How Florida got the players they got, and there was controversy about one kid from Tennessee [Corey Brewer] that maybe we could have gotten. He was a really good player. People couldn't understand how Florida had better players than Kentucky.

LEACH: And you had Chris Lofton, a Kentucky kid from Mason County, shooting the lights out for Tennessee and winning SEC Player of the Year honors in 2007. I can understand fans who cite him as a recruiting mistake. He was clearly good enough to play here and should have been a Wildcat. When I would go for the pregame interviews, I would get there early and talk with Bill Keightley, and the topics were usually Kentucky high school basketball or the Cincinnati Reds. I guarantee you that if "Mr. Wildcat" were still with us and read that statement about Chris Lofton, he would be shaking his head in affirmation although he would have never publicly criticized a UK coach. More so than great dunkers, I think Kentucky fans love great shooters, and there were not many from this state that shot the ball better than him.

PRATT: Boy, he had a quick release. He's as good a shooter as I've ever seen.

LEACH: Missing out on Lofton added to the pressure and the discontent among fans. Under the best of circumstances, this job is demanding, and when your team doesn't meet expectations and things aren't going well, it can really weigh heavily on you. And do you think the way recruiting was changing, with one-and-done just about to heat up, was something that Tubby was a little reluctant to incorporate into his program?

PRATT: I think the world changed on Tubby. He was really good at finding guys who were talented but maybe overlooked and he would polish them up. Meeks was not a guy that overly recruited but Dave Hobbs got in there early and signed him—and you knew he was going to take a big step the next year. But the change in recruiting, the one-and-done, how quickly can you take me to the NBA, that wasn't Tubby. He was a patient, let-me-coach-you guy and then you'll get there. All that chatter is part of the stuff that goes around a team. It was bad then and it's worse now with social media and that just doesn't help your team-building process. It may hurt in some situations, if you know what I mean. There's certain things that can be addressed and dealt with as a coach and other things from outside influences that you can't deal with. You try, but good luck with that one. I don't think Tubby felt comfortable [with how the recruiting landscape changed].

LEACH: I always thought Tubby could have adapted if he had stayed, and he was such a good coach that he would have had good teams. Jodie Meeks was a freshman on that '07 team, and I think he was a classic Tubby kind of player in terms of being mentally tough. Jodie provided one of the highlights of that season in coming off the bench for 18 in an unexpected win at Louisville. You put him with Patrick Patterson the next year and those two could have been the building blocks for a resurgence for Tubby.

PRATT: I agree. I think he would have put Jodie and Patrick on the same side of the floor and say, "Who are you gonna guard?" I know how he looked at the offense and he would have utilized those guys really well. Hobbs had found Jodie down at the Peach Jam before his senior year and said, "We gotta have this guy." A day later, he goes back to see him and every assistant in the SEC was there.

LEACH: Hard to find those under-the-radar guys anymore. We'll never know how it would have played out, but I do know we both hated to see Tubby leave because he was as good a man as you'll ever find and he was a pleasure to work with.

PRATT: No question. I go back to when he coached Hoke County High School and I was a snot-nosed assistant coach at UNC–Charlotte, and he had a kid that I tried to recruit. Then he was with J. D. Barnett at VCU. He and Hobbs were up there with J. D., so we were all in the Sun Belt Conference. Tubby was a friend of mine, a friend of yours, and he was good to work with, and whenever I'd call him up and say, "Tub man, can I come by practice?" He'd say, "Come by practice and stop by the office early." So I'd go chat with him and then I'd go to practice. He was a really good man, and a good man to work with.

LEACH: As good a man as you'll ever find. He is appreciated for the quality of person that he is, but I think underappreciated for his coaching. Again, maybe following Rick and then some recruiting issues at the end caused fans to turn sour. But when he came back in later years to be honored in the UK Hall of Fame, it warmed my heart to see how fans embraced him. What an incredible ovation he received at the football game when they announced the Hall of Famers in his year.

PRATT: Absolutely. And he came to Louisville a couple of years ago for this golf outing and he and I spent a lot of time talking post-golf and boy, the people who came up to him and wanted to talk to him, and I watched him during the course of the two days and people came up and they wanted to talk to Tubby, they really respected Tubby. He did well by the University of Kentucky basketball program, there's no question.

2008

This was probably the strangest season we covered—and that includes the pandemic year. Things went south pretty quickly for new coach Billy Gillispie when the Wildcats were upset by Gardner-Webb in the second game. Shortly thereafter, there was a stretch of four losses in five games, culminating in a home court loss to San Diego, dropping the record to 5-6. But then, starting on January 22 with an upset of third-ranked Tennessee, they went on a stretch of nine wins in 10 games—however, the one loss was a 41-pointer at Vandy in which they were down 41-11 at halftime. At the end of that stretch, Patrick Patterson was lost for the season to an injury, and even though they nearly upset Tennessee again in the first game without him, the season was pretty much done at that point. And of course, the capper to that season with the famous "tornado game" at the SEC Tournament when they lost to Georgia in overtime.

LEACH: When did you first think that Billy might not be a good fit at UK?

PRATT: The first time I questioned it was shortly after he was hired, I called a former player of mine who was an assistant coach. He had worked at Texas A&M and he had heard when Billy took over the Aggies that when he did his radio show, he sometimes didn't show up. He had hard times with the administration there too. He said people over there didn't like him. They were happy for him to go because he treated people badly. That's the first time I thought, "Well, this isn't going to be good if he's not going to be fan friendly with Big Blue Nation." From there, I got to watch practice and I didn't like the way he treated the players. He was so negative with them. He coached from a negative point all the time, it seemed like. These guys, they were used to Tubby. He was a driver who pushed his players, but he didn't do it negatively. It was hard to get a compliment out of Billy in practice. I don't know if he thought he was Bob Knight Jr. or what. In the very first year I thought that if somebody watches practice and they're being recruited, and that prospect gets put with some of these players, Billy was gonna have a hard time because the players were probably not gonna help him recruit. So those were the two pieces: the June comment from a guy I trust and when I actually got to watch his practices and what went on. I think Billy demotivated guys.

LEACH: Fans didn't have that perspective that you did so I think the alarm bells for them went off with that loss to Gardner-Webb. Kentucky was struggling from the start, but I told our producer, Mike Dodson, that they would eventually make a run. Then, around the first media timeout of the second half, I turned to him and said, "It ain't happening tonight." Gardner-Webb was just beating them on a backdoor play time and time again. Looking back at that box score, I had forgotten one interesting note—it was the best game for Alex Legion in a very short stay. The next strange loss came about a month later, when UAB beat them at Freedom Hall. A former Indiana man, Robert Vaden, lit them up for 33 points and Billy's stubborn streak showed up when he never used anyone but Michael Porter to guard him. I know you got a kick out of his answer when I asked him about that strategy in the postgame show.

PRATT: I didn't typically stay there for the coach interview. I'd just get in my car and go home, but I decided to stay around because I was interested in what he would say because he made no changes in guarding Vaden, who was having a lights-out game. I think we talked about it off air and I hung around on purpose to hear what he would have to say about that. What was his response?

LEACH: "That wasn't what beat us."

PRATT: Yep. That was exactly it.

LEACH: You disputed that notion, right? [laughs]

PRATT: Absolutely. I mean, the guy goes for what, 35? The total points they scored, he got almost half their points: 35 out of 79. And that wasn't the problem. [laughs again] He kept Porter on him most of the night. Poor kid. He shot over the top of him and drove by him. It was like Porter was on an island. I felt sorry for the kid.

LEACH: They did regroup in conference play, beat a 13th-ranked Vandy team and a Tennessee club that was top three at the time, and that generated some hope for getting the season back on track. But once they lost Patrick Patterson to that injury late in the season, I think they were done, and probably the most memorable thing about the remainder of that season was the "tornado game" at the SEC Tournament in Atlanta. That was bizarre. You and I were sitting there on Friday night waiting to do the Kentucky-Georgia game and they had us do the end of the Mississippi State–Alabama game on the network and it went to overtime. You and I just kinda called that while we were filling time. I can't even remember who won, but that game going into overtime probably saved lives by keeping fans in the arena rather than spilling out on the streets just as a tornado was hitting downtown Atlanta.

PRATT: I remember looking up at the boom that comes over for the camera and it was moving erratically and I'm thinking, "What the hell is going on?" Then maybe somebody told us to crawl under the table on press row. I don't think we did that, but I looked around and saw a hole in the roof. That was a wild night.

Then we went to Georgia Tech to play Georgia, and they had family and friends, just a very, very small crowd. I don't think our guys wanted to play, and they got beat in overtime by a very mediocre Georgia team. There's no way in hell that team was better than Kentucky. If we had played on Friday night, there's no question we would have won the game, but all that stuff going on, the limited crowd, etc.

LEACH: The media shuttles weren't running that night, so we walked back to the UK hotel and saw all the broken windows in those office buildings. And I went to sleep late that night not knowing what the plan was for the next day, and when I woke up, I saw a text from Scott Stricklin of UK media relations about the move to Tech, and I remember having to hustle to get packed up and get over there.

PRATT: That was such a strange situation. We had a limited offense and Joe and Ramel had to try and carry the show for that team. That was a tough way to lose a ballgame. There's no way in hell that team was better than Kentucky. If we had played on Friday night, I think there's no question Kentucky would have won the game.

LEACH: The season probably should have ended there—an odd game to end an odd season—but they got into the NCAA Tournament as an 11-seed. Joe Crawford had a huge game, but Marquette was just better, and it was over. I know that last season at UK wasn't much for Joe and Ramel Bradley, but I thought they showed amazing mental toughness and leadership.

PRATT: I think you found out those guys were winners and they were willing to compete to do that. Ramel was really a good point guard, and when Joe got to taking that ball to rim, boy, was he was aggressive. And Patrick Patterson came in far ahead, really polished for a freshman, the way he conducted himself and the way he played. Very mature.

LEACH: It's also worth noting that Jodie got hurt early in that season and he really didn't get to show what he could do.

PRATT: Yes. He had the sports hernia. I thought Billy's offense was structurally good, but I thought the way he treated the players—I thought, "How are you gonna get anything out of them?" Then when he treated Jodie the way he did. The kid played hard and all of that kinda stuff that you need but man, the way Billy treated him about that injury. Do you remember going to LSU? That game determined whether he could be redshirted or not, and Billy didn't play him in the first half, then he played him in the second. I don't know if Jodie would have gone for the redshirt thing or not, I never asked him, but I remember that game down in Baton Rouge. I kept thinking he didn't put him in the first half so he's not well and then all of a sudden, Billy pops him in the second half, which blew away the chance to redshirt.

LEACH: And Derrick Jasper was hurt too, and we never got to see the best of his game.

PRATT: Billy totally misused that kid. I always liked Derrick's potential—a big wing, a point forward, or guard. I know he struggled with the knee. He never was the same. I always liked Jasper. He would have been a Calipari-type point guard. He knew how to go places.

LEACH: There's one other funny story from that season. I was with the football team at the Music City Bowl and a group of us were watching the basketball game at a sports bar in Nashville early in the day when I got a text from Brian Lane, the Transy coach who I've known from his high school days at Tates Creek. After Neil Price did the pregame interview with Billy, the text said something like, "Billy likes the new guy better" and I got a good laugh out of that.

Billy and I had some unusual interviews, especially early in that first season. He seemed to like to play what I would call mind games with you. I would try to engage him in conversation during the Monday night shows, but he was just staring at his phone, so I gave up after a few tries. But in February something unexpected happened, and from that point on, we had a much better working relationship than it sometimes sounded on the air. We happened to be walking out the door at the same time and I mentioned a horse named Pyro that had scored an impressive win in a Kentucky Derby prep, knowing that Billy was a big Thoroughbred racing fan. His eyes lit up and we stood there in the parking lot talking horses for 15–20 minutes. He knows racing and loved talking about it.

2009

With two players as good as Jodie Meeks and Patrick Patterson, this team should have been better than it was— and in fact, through 20 games, it was very good, with only four losses. And then came the famous "Jeanine Edwards bad question" moment at Ole Miss. Billy Gillispie responded in a rude manner to Edwards's question on the ESPN telecast about Jodie Meeks's lack of first-half production, and Kentucky went on to lose a game it had led at halftime. Gillispie's treatment of Edwards became the bigger story, however. That loss at Ole Miss turned out to start a streak in which UK lost three games in a row and eight of its next 11 heading into the SEC Tournament, culminating with a Senior Night loss to a bad Georgia team. The Wildcats ended up in the NIT, where they won two games before ending the season—and the Gillispie era—with a loss at Notre Dame.

LEACH: VMI beat them 111-103 in the first game and that kinda set the tone for that season—Jodie would score a lot and the team would have some very disappointing losses. In the mindset of all that turmoil, Jodie Meeks had an incredible season. Let's start with the 54-point game at Tennessee. We were chatting with our buddy Bob Kesling [voice of the Vols] before the game and he pointed to a young manager and said that young man had played Meeks's role in a scrimmage the day before and got 36 points, so we thought the potential was there for Jodie to do well—just not 54 points well.

PRATT: He had 46 earlier in the year at Freedom Hall [against

Appalachian State], and I remember him coming out postgame to talk to us and I wanted to congratulate him. He didn't know that he had broken my record. He just looked at me—he had a big smile on his face—and he gave me a fist bump. Then to watch him go to work and to break Dan Issel's record [for most points in a single game by a UK player]. He turned up off those picks on the base line much like Tyler Herro. He cut tight and he knew when to turn on the gas; when he got the guy behind that pick, he would turn up and *bam!* Catch and shoot, which was his bag. That was an unbelievable performance. Of course, I was there when Issel set it, set the record, and I'd already been taken out of the game down in Mississippi. Mississippi was the weakest team in the league at that time. I was already out for whatever reason, and Dan was going about his stuff and somebody on the bench, I don't know whether it was Russell Rice, somebody had told the bench before I got back there that Issel's on this record-setting pace so we all kinda knew. Then somebody said when he broke the record and that was neat. He did it differently, obviously, because he played a different position than Jodie, but he would score and get fouled and it was just like, man, these guys gotta quit fouling this cat. [*laughter*]

LEACH: When Meeks had 49 points and was going to the free-throw line, a Tennessee player who had been trash-talking the whole night [while Meeks was lighting him up, mind you] was on the free-throw lane next to Jodie. So Jodie leans over and says the only thing he said all night—"Hey, [expletive]. In case you lost count, this is 50." I remember you, me, and Jim Barnhart driving back home the next day, and Dan called you to talk about Jodie's performance.

PRATT: He said he had called Jodie or was getting ready to call. We talked about how Jodie scored his points and we laughed about how Dan scored his points and he was very, very happy for Jodie. That's a big record now!

LEACH: Patrick Patterson showed a lot of mental toughness in that crazy season, on a team having to deal with a lot of distractions.

PRATT: Patrick had a high basketball IQ. He knew the game and he knew what he could do and how to plug it in and—I say this as a compliment—he knew how to get easy baskets. Patrick knew: he would move his feet, he would find the rebound, get the putback. He knew how to maximize his offense and find those easier hoops, for lack of a better terminology.

LEACH: That sour end to the regular season put Kentucky in the NIT but that did give you and me a memorable moment to savor in doing a postseason game at Memorial Coliseum. The game was moved there because Rupp Arena was hosting the state high school tournament. You played your whole career in that building and it's where I saw my first UK basketball game. A dear friend of my dad's [a guy named John Wall, ironically] had season tickets and would take my dad and me to a few games each season so it was special to have a chance to work a game in that building with such significance, even if it was just the NIT. And the crowd that night was amazing.

PRATT: People got into that game who usually couldn't get in, and that made it a terrific crowd. And then Lon Kruger, I think that was one of his last teams at UNLV. I always thought the guy was a terrific coach. That crowd got the team over the hump. Losing five of the last six, and the fans were excited about being there, seeing a game there, and knew that might be history—they got this team over the hump, I thought.

LEACH: Absolutely. I just loved watching games in Memorial Coliseum and part of it is maybe when you're younger, you romanticize, but it seemed like with that flat rough in the Coliseum, you could feel the building shake when it got loud. When you guys were playing and you'd run down that ramp onto the court from the hall that came out of the locker room. The Cats came out and the fight song started. The place shook and to be in that atmosphere again to some extent was a lot of fun.

PRATT: Our locker room was back in the back and underneath the stands, and then they had the gates they kept closed. Once we went back for the final gathering before we came out, they shut the gates. And I was told by the people who were on the outside looking in, they knew we were coming out of the locker room, down that hall that kinda wound around, but once they opened the gates, the fans knew that we were coming out. That got them excited that we came out of the tunnel. Recently, I walked out to see something in the Coliseum, and I just stood there and looked at the place and thought, "Man, there were a lot of great feelings in this place." I played there and then I broadcast the last men's game there and that's really cool.

LEACH: Kentucky had an exciting win in the second round of the NIT at Creighton, 65-63. Meeks converted a 3-point play in the final seconds to give the Cats the win. It was a tremendous atmosphere—great fans who probably knew this would be the only time they would see their team in a home game against the University of Kentucky. But the season ended at the next stop, at Notre Dame, and the rumors were flying about a possible coaching change. And you had already had an indication earlier that a change might be coming, right?

PRATT: There was a lot of controversy and late in the year, Mitch Barnhart came by the broadcast table and said he wanted to talk to me. He called me soon after and said, "What do you think is going on?" I told him, "Billy is a solid coach, but I don't think he'll get out of his players what he should get out of them"—and Jodie was one of the focal points. I told Mitch that I had watched practice and it was organized and all, but Billy was so negative with these kids, and I didn't think that was good. And there were stories about how he had treated Josh Harrelson and Darius Miller poorly, and those things bothered me because those guys were good kids. He was taking away a large portion of their happiness in playing, and you've got to feel about good about yourself and what you're doing. And then the discussion got to recruiting and how we were struggling. He didn't tell me he wanted to fire Billy or anything. It was just a discussion of what was going on.

LEACH: But by the time we were up in South Bend for that Notre Dame game, it was clear where things were headed with Billy, and so I guess you were drafted to help with the search, right?

PRATT: I was doing a workout on a treadmill and the story hits the news with Mitch doing a press conference, and somebody asked him who was going to be on the committee for the search. Mitch mentioned Dr. Todd, and [assistant AD] Rob Mullens and me, and I said, "What?" I didn't think I was going to be brought into the picture publicly. I didn't mind but then my phone blew up. Mitch had said he didn't want names to get out and so my wife was answering the phone and telling everyone that I was not available.

LEACH: I knew his backstory of you being involved in the coaching search, but I didn't call you for info. I wasn't going to betray your confidence and break any stories, and I knew you were getting swamped with calls. But at some point very early in this process, Calipari's name gets put into the mix—and that's probably the best point at which to start the next chapter.

2010

An upset loss to West Virginia in the Elite Eight was a disappointing way to end the 2010 season, but a 35-3 record, with some big wins along the way, had put the fun back in the UK basketball program for the BBN. Kentucky was the "it" program again, probably for the first time since that long winning streak in 2003. And the man responsible for that was John Calipari, along with the players he brought into the Kentucky program, who really connected with the fans. So the recap of this season must start with how Calipari came to be the coach.

LEACH: As long as you've been involved in the game and the contacts you've made, it was inevitable that prospective coaches would reach out to you in some fashion, especially once they knew you were part of the team that would help identify candidates for this prestigious job. How did John Calipari's name get on the table for this search?

PRATT: Memphis had gotten beat [in the NCAA Tournament], and I get a call from Dave Pendergraft [who worked on Calipari's staff in the NBA]. He said, "Cal wanted me to call you," and Dave said, "Cal wants the job." He was selling me on Calipari, and I said, "You don't need to." I never said to Mitch that one of Cal's buddies called but, I said, "Cal really wants the job," and I knew that was big to Mitch and Dr. Todd. They wanted to get the deal done [with the next coach] and not have to go through a long, drawn-out type of thing.

LEACH: You were part of the group that flew on a private plane to have the first meeting with Cal, right?

PRATT: Mitch said they were getting some pushback on Calipari and he said, "You've got to talk to Dr. Todd. He likes you. He knows you. He went to school with Gary Gamble, one of your teammates." So Lee Todd and I had a great conversation and he had a lot of questions and I said, "Ask Calipari about any issues you have and see what he says." I told him the guy really wants to coach at Kentucky, he understands it. I told Cal didn't have the support system at Memphis or UMass that he would have here with Sandy Bell [to monitor compliance issues, boosters, etc.]. So we go meet with Cal and we're there for three or four hours. Lee Todd had all kinds of questions and Cal addressed them straight on. I've seen a lot of sales presentations and Cal was terrific. He answered everything and then he got a chance to sell himself.

LEACH: What stood out about what Cal making his pitch for the job?

PRATT: He knew the hot buttons. He had studied the program. He understood the relationship between the coach and the fans. And he talked about recruiting the best of the best. He said, "You're not doing that," and I always remember this line—he said, "When I walk in now and they say Kentucky is talking to them, I have no worries. Most of the kids I hear that Kentucky is after, I'm not recruiting them." Cal was sitting in a chair with the back to the wall and the four of us are listening to him and he said, "Dr. Todd, if you hire me to coach Kentucky and Rick Pitino finds out and he's asleep, this is how he's going to be when he wakes up," and Cal put his hands up in the air like he was nervous [*imitates how he imagined Pitino would react*]. On the way home, I talked with Lee Todd some more and I felt really good. Everybody had somebody they were championing, and there was one person that was pushing Billy Donovan. I told Mitch, "He [Billy Donovan] is not coming." I was friends with Don Dizney [a Florida booster who was close to Donovan], and Don told me Billy wasn't coming because he didn't want to compete with Pitino. I said, "Let's go get Cal." I think the one thing that really helped a lot was how Mitch got strung along last time [in the search for Tubby's successor] and when he left that meeting with Calipari, he knew Calipari really wanted the job.

LEACH: We need to take a detour in this discussion for a minute and talk about the other candidate that reached out to you through an intermediary.

PRATT: Billy Reed [a veteran Kentucky journalist] is a good friend of mine. I wasn't taking any calls like that, but I had to call Billy back. He said, "Mike, I don't want you to be offended by what I'm going to say, but I need to do this for another friend of mine." I said, "Billy, who is it?" and he said, "Bob Knight." I said, "You're kidding me." Bob Knight had Billy Reed call me to say he was interested in the job. The next time I saw Mitch, I told him about the call. I don't think Mitch wanted another Bobby Knight because he just got rid of one.

LEACH: We talked about why you thought Billy was not going to be a good fit for Kentucky. Why did you think the matchup with Cal and Kentucky basketball was going to work so well?

PRATT: Cal had some of the same traits Pitino had. He understood the fan base. He could relate to them in many ways. He understood the history of the program. He had played Kentucky when he was at UMass. So he had a good feel, not just from afar but he had actually been in the game with Kentucky to feel the fan base and those kinds of things that you have to get a feel for.

LEACH: I thought he had a better feeling for the fans and the history of the place than even Rick did. How he connected with Joe B. shortly after getting hired, and he seemed to be welcoming to former players more than Rick was. And It had to be quite a change when you went to practices and watched John Wall, DeMarcus Cousins, and Eric Bledsoe after what you'd been watching previously.

PRATT: The thing that jumped out at me the most was the athleticism and the competitiveness. Patrick Patterson pretty much had his way in practice and wasn't really pushed by anybody [under Gillispie], but when Cal came, there was a big difference in practices. Big difference.

LEACH: As you reflect on that first season under Calipari, do you remember when you started to think that team was going to have one of those special years?

PRATT: I remember the first game with Miami of Ohio—John Wall won it for us on a buzzer shot. I thought that was good to see from a kid you expected to deliver as a go-to guy in that year. Patrick could get it done inside, but we didn't have a guard coming back who could score a basket like that. I thought that was a big sign. And when we beat North Carolina I thought that was a big sign too.

LEACH: Both teams were top 10, and it had been quite awhile since Rupp Arena had that "big-game buzz" with a packed house, anticipating a big win. Kentucky went on a long run, like 20-2 that John Wall keyed, and I don't think it had been that loud since that 2003 team upset number one Florida. That day was when I thought Kentucky basketball is back where it needs to be.

PRATT: I would agree. That was about six, eight games into the year and fans decided they liked this team because the team won every game. And they followed up with a tight one with UConn.

LEACH: That was fun for me from a broadcasting standpoint. It wasn't like it is set up now for the Champions Classic games at Madison Square Garden, and so our broadcast spot was down there courtside, and for me it was fun to be able to work a game from that location in that building because one of my first favorite teams growing up was the New York Knicks with Walt Frazier, Earl "the Pearl" Monroe, and the rest. John Wall was spectacular in that game against UConn, and they were honoring legendary players that had played in the Garden, and Oscar Robertson was in the crowd so that was a fun night, to see a high-level game and be courtside at the Garden to call it. The Cats were rolling at that point, and the next big game was the one against Louisville. Calipari's arrival certainly put the energy back in that rivalry.

PRATT: It was an electric atmosphere for that first game. I remember a story where one of the Louisville guys was yapping at Bledsoe and finally Calipari is standing there and he says to the player something to the effect of "Son, you're picking on the wrong guy." Bledsoe was built like a linebacker, and this guy didn't have the physique to be challenging Bledsoe.

LEACH: Kentucky steamrolled through the regular season. Took their first loss down at South Carolina where they just lost their focus a little bit. Sometimes the game day practices—shootarounds, they're called—can be an indication of a team that is really sharp or also distracted, and that was a day when there was more goofing around at the shootaround, and they were upset later that night. Then they lost at Tennessee. A lot of good Kentucky teams have lost in Knoxville, and that was just a bad day at the office. The Cats came back and beat Tennessee in the SEC Tournament just a few weeks later, 74-45, which I thought was a pretty clear signal of what they were capable of and how focused they were at that time.

PRATT: Wasn't it the South Carolina game when Obama called the team and Big Cuz [Demarcus Cousins] talked to him? And I remember that Mississippi State game in the tournament championship.

LEACH: Oh, yeah. They had played Kentucky really tough down in Starkville. It was an overtime game. They were throwing stuff on the floor as Kentucky left. There were some calls that didn't go State's way and their fans were upset. State was older and they played Kentucky tough, but the last-second putback by Cousins gave UK its first SEC Tournament title since '04 and the BBN party was on in Nashville. Then it was on to the NCAA Tournament.

They cruised down there in New Orleans, got up to Syracuse, played Cornell, and they went cold in the second half. I recall they did not make a single "three" in the second half. It's funny how that can happen sometimes to an entire team—where they just go cold—because obviously it carried over to West Virginia.

PRATT: Even though Kentucky went cold, they still won by 17 [over Cornell], and then West Virginia played that 1-3-1 zone. We didn't do a good job of cracking that one. We settled for that long three-point shot.

LEACH: Kentucky ended up four of 32. That was 32 threes out of 67 overall field goal attempts, and that's never what Cal wants. They just got sucked into that zone.

PRATT: They were 0 for 20 in the first half. They took 32 for the night, so they were four of 12 in the second half. That's 33 percent. That's livable, but you buried yourself with that first half. Cal made an adjustment in the second half against the 1-3-1—he started picking the back guy on the 1-3-1 and tried to work it into Big Cuz. It presented some opportunities for Cuz and he took advantage, but we couldn't guard the little guard.

LEACH: Joe Mazzulla. Scored 17.

PRATT: They loved him off that high pick and roll. He'd turn the corner and head down that lane. We didn't communicate well on that play. Ran it over and over. Once he got the paint touch, man, he was crafty finishing at the basket, or he would kick for the three. I remember that. That's the game, and I think I told you all year long about Jodie Meeks, that Jodie would be the icing on the cake. All year long we had that discussion and I really believed it.

LEACH: I don't think that zone would have worked nearly as well with Jodie Meeks on the floor. You thought Jodie was just a little uncertain about playing for a third different coach in his career. He had all those huge numbers, and it was safer to just go to the league.

PRATT: His dad told me that, matter of fact. Jodie's dad said, "Look, we came to Kentucky because of David Hobbs and Tubby Smith. So then they're gone and we have Billy Clyde, who didn't recruit us, but we stayed with it because Jodie was happy. So now we've got a third coach in three years, we didn't think it was in our best interest because the people we came there for—Tubby and Hobbs—weren't there." Later on, Calipari tells me that [veteran NBA coach and Calipari friend] Larry Brown told him, "You don't need Jodie with what you've got, and he's not gonna play in the NBA anyway." I think Cal wins a championship right out of the shoot with Jodie Meeks at the wing.

LEACH: It was disappointing because I remember Kansas had gotten upset and Duke ended up winning the title. I thought Kentucky was way better than Duke that year, but when West Virginia upset Kentucky, it just kinda fell together for Duke. I thought Kansas. Back to the West Virginia game, did you think Kentucky's players panicked a little when they could sense their season slipping away from them?

PRATT: Yeah, they were playing all those young guys and I think they did [panic].

2011

The Enes Kanter storyline dominated the off-season, as he was viewed by fans as the key piece to the Wildcats getting the title they had missed out on the year before, but when the NCAA ruling went against him, some of the air came out of the bubble. Kentucky fans tend to mark the potential of their teams by how they perform in the early marquee games, and when this group suffered a lopsided loss to UConn in Maui and a two-pointer at North Carolina, there was some frustration, even though the team was winning all of the other games. As the conference season unfolded, Kentucky suffered several close losses, but the coaches and players figured it out late and started to jell in the final week of the regular season.

PRATT: "Jonesy" [Terrence Jones] got off to a pretty good start then he hit the wall. He really struggled, and of course he came in with all the hype, but Brandon Knight, that guy could score the ball. He could score and he wasn't a bad passer but he was a scoring point guard, there's no question about that. That was kind of a funny team. Nobody thought that team would be any good. Do you remember why? Nobody had much respect for Harrelson or Liggins.

LEACH: They had Kanter that they were hoping to get eligible and he never got eligible, so they thought their chance was gone without Enes. Josh was a great story because I go back to that game out in Vegas in his first year in 2008, and that was a game where he showed you he had something to his game. He never got much of a chance after that with Billy and then that first year with Cousins and those guys he never really got any run with Cal, and I think he surprised the coaches with what he did.

PRATT: He didn't have much of a track record going into that season. The kid had a soft touch, and he knew how to play. He wasn't a great athlete—but the kid knew how to play.

LEACH: Calipari did a nice job using Josh as an unconventional center. He wasn't the back to the basket five man. They used him away from the basket some. You had a guy like Terrance who was strong posting up and just let Josh do what he could do best, get rebounds, set screens, make a shot when it was open, and then they ended up getting a lot more than they thought they would get out of him.

PRATT: He was really good at going to set the pick and then slipping to the basket or setting the pick and then fading for the jump shot—he got really good at that.

LEACH: They ran a lot of that high pick and roll with Brandon, started to run the offense through him. You had Josh, who set really good screens, Brandon knew how to use them, and then he had Josh that he could pick and pop with, so you had to respect Josh rolling off that screen and that combo—the way those two played off each other really drove a lot of that team's success.

PRATT: No question. If they switched, they had a mismatch. Josh on the small guy, but then the big guy couldn't guard Knight off the pick, and it was a tough situation for them. Then if they went behind on Knight, he could jump up and shoot it and make it, so you had to adjust your defense on that based upon how people were playing in that particular game.

LEACH: You didn't know who your center was gonna be because Enes didn't get eligible, you had some highly regarded freshmen but not as highly regarded as John Wall and Cuz. Deandre was a nice story. He hit a shot late in the Carolina game. A big three that kinda clinched it. Calipari gave him a kiss on the forehead. Deandre was a great story those first couple years for Cal in that he and Billy got crossways and Cal gave him a chance at a fresh start and DeAndre really embraced it.

PRATT: That was good to see for all the reasons you just mentioned. The kid embraced it because he wanted to play defense. Ultimately, he did the one thing people said he couldn't do and really he had not done, and that was shoot that three-point shot when left alone. I thought all along he would be a player that would fit for Calipari, particularly defensively, because he could take it to the rim and get out in transition and could D it up. The one that surprised me that played so well that year for Calipari was Josh. I just didn't see him fitting into the Calipari mold but Kanter can't play and Jones is really a forward so Josh stepped in and played well.

LEACH: When they lost another close game out at Arkansas, I remember telling you that it wasn't going to happen for this team because they could not win a close game. But they came back to play a good Vandy team and their shootaround that day was maybe the best one of the year and they won a close game. Then the same thing happened against Florida and at Tennessee, so they finish with three wins in the regular season. Go down, win the SEC Tournament convincingly, beat Florida by 16 in the final. Then they go down to Tampa and nearly got knocked out in the first round by Princeton.

PRATT: I remember in the broadcast we talked about how he made that shot, Knight makes that shot. He's driving as the game is winding down, he's driving to the hoop. The Princeton guy comes over and he thinks he can block that shot and he goes up to block it right where you should block it, he's gonna pin it on the glass. High up on the glass where he thinks that Brandon is gonna shoot the ball from. Then Brandon scoops him, scoops under him. It was such a heady play. So I'm in the lobby after the game and Brandon comes down and he's waiting for somebody and I started talking to him. I said, "Man, that was one of the smartest plays I've ever seen.

Did you know where that guy was?" He said, "Yeah, I felt him. I just knew he was there and I figured he was gonna go for the block and I just scooped him." And that's what he did. That was a really amazing play because he did it by feeling.

LEACH: That was the only basket he made in that game. He was one for eight. And then against Ohio State, he hits the game winner and at the moment he took the shot, he was three for nine. He's the kinda player coaches always talk about. Cal says the key to being a great clutch shooter is you can't be afraid to take 'em, and he loved takin' 'em. He missed several of them during the regular season, but he was huge in the postseason. In that game, he hit the one against Ohio State. He had the mentality for being the guy you wanted to have the ball at the end, no matter what he'd done during the game. He clearly never lost confidence. He makes that one against Princeton and again, that's the only basket he makes. And then Ohio State, tie game, he goes off the pick and roll there and goes to the elbow and hits the shot against Ohio State when he had seven points at that point in the night.

PRATT: Didn't Liggins have a big game defensively? And Harrelson battled their big guy [All-American Jared Sullinger].

LEACH: The thing I remember about Ohio State, Josh set a tone early when he fired that ball off Sullinger that Kentucky wasn't backing down. They had the mindset you had to have to beat a team like Ohio State. And after they beat Ohio State I really felt like they were in a place with their confidence where they were not gonna be denied getting to the Final Four.

PRATT: I thought after beating Princeton, "This team's got some juice." But that was a damn tough regional.

LEACH: Coaches talk sometimes about teams gaining momentum during the tournament, and that's what happened to that Kentucky team. They'd won three close games in a row. So they get to the Final Four and run into Connecticut and just shot it so poorly.

Brandon was six of 23. Every team shot poorly down there. It just seemed like a bad shooting environment.

PRATT: We had a hard time with Kemba Walker. He had 29 when they played in Maui and then when they played in the Final Four, Kentucky defended him better; he was six of 15 but he still had 18 points and seven assists. He was just a tough guard. Still, with Kentucky struggling, they end up losing by one. Four of 12 from the free-throw line killed 'em. Remember, there was Butler and VCU on the other side. None of the teams were expected to be there. It was there for the taking. Nice run for Kentucky. As the season played out they had a viable chance to win the national championship, and they weren't anywhere as close to as good as the team before or a couple after them, but they nearly pulled it off. I would say that year was probably as rewarding as any to the Big Blue Nation and to Calipari.

LEACH: If you don't have Kemba Walker on the other team, you get by that game and you win the championship. They could have easily started with two. The previous year he had a much better team that didn't get to the Final Four, and then in 2011, that was celebrated by the Kentucky fans because they hadn't been to a Final Four since the championship in '98. They were good enough to go in '03, '04, good enough to go in 2010, but didn't get there in any of those years, and then to finally get there when it really wasn't expected was really special.

PRATT: Making it to the Final Four his first year and then the second year making it to the Final Four and then the championship the next year, do you think that spoiled Kentucky people because of the point you make, they hadn't been there for such a long time? Now all of a sudden they think we're gonna go every year or every other year.

LEACH: Maybe so especially when you add in '14 and unexpected run, then '15, you're so good and at that point fans don't appreciate fully how hard it is to get to those spots in the tournament. In those years, that run, a lot of things broke Kentucky's way. It seemed to break the other way in '17 and '19 seasons.

PRATT: It was like, we put up with Billy Clyde and all the frustration that went with him and all of a sudden here comes this guy Calipari, and right from the start you can feel pretty comfortable dreaming about going to the Final Four. So getting off to that kind of start as a coach—because in all honesty, we all thought because of what Billy didn't leave or left, that it was going to be a rebuilding deal—and all of a sudden Cal brings in these guys Wall, Cousins, Bledsoe, and he's left with a really good player in Patrick Patterson who's willing to subjugate himself to a different role and away you go. It was amazing timing.

LEACH: So they're coming off a big year in 2010 and you're thinking it might be a big bounce down and then they got a surprising Final Four out of it. When you and I started, you think you're gonna be in the Final Four in '03, '04 you're the number one seed, then '05 you're not the best team, but Duke got upset and you're there at the regional final and you think when you're a Kentucky announcer you're gonna be going to Final Fours from time to time and then we missed three years in a row there when it was possible, so by the time it finally happened in 2011, those final moments of the win over North Carolina in the regional final were memorable. And it was fun for us to get to go to a Final Four and call a Kentucky game there on that stage.

2012

This was a year like the ones in 1996 and 1978 in that Kentucky had a good shot to win a national title in the preceding year but came up short, and now the expectations bar was set at its highest level. Those '96 and '78 teams played in an era when players didn't leave school so early, so this was a different set of circumstances, but you still had a good bit of carryover in the return of players like Doron Lamb, Terrence Jones, and Darius Miller, and they were added to a freshman class led by the number one recruit in Anthony Davis—and he was as good as advertised.

LEACH: The win over Kansas at Madison Square Garden was noteworthy, but for me the statement win early in that season was the one over Carolina at Rupp in early December. When Davis blocked that shot [by John Henson, in the final seconds], I always thought, that was one of the loudest moments I've heard at Rupp Arena. If you're ranking it, that's somewhere in the top five. To cover the space he covered with a guy that tall with those long arms—it was just an incredible play.

PRATT: He went across the lane and he got there, and his momentum didn't carry him into the shooter, John Henson, who's six eight, six nine, but his momentum didn't carry him into Henson to make the foul. He went across the lane, went straight up and blocked the shot when it left his hand. And that was it, man. We were ranked one, they were ranked five, and that was one helluva basketball game.

LEACH: As the season wore on, I thought Kentucky or Carolina would win the title. Some years there are several teams in that top tier but that year, for me, it was hard to imagine anyone else was on their level.

PRATT: Louisville was pretty good that year and when we played them, they were in the top five. I thought Kansas was good, Carolina, Louisville, that was a heck of a December for basketball games.

LEACH: The week after the Carolina game, we go up to Indiana, and I remember you, me, and Jim Barnhart drove to Bloomington. We were taking the equipment in and all of those students were lined up to get inside. They usually don't pay much attention to us, but they were so juiced up that I remember it felt different. The feeling you got, the vibe from how strong the students reacted to us, much less the team. Early on you thought this is gonna be a challenging environment.

PRATT: They were taunting us as we walked in.

LEACH: [*laughter*] The radio crew doesn't normally get that.

PRATT: Once we got inside and got set up it was the second cut above the benches and the good seats were the second cut, so then you had to walk across the basketball floor to get to the pressroom. The students and fans were on that side of the floor and they were cussing us. When we walked back out on the floor from the pressroom they were hollering and cussing. It had been a long time since I'd seen fans that ugly. Like it was really important to mess with us! [*laughter*] We're just the radio guys. That was a lot like some of the crowds we faced when I played. The Tennessee and the Vanderbilt's, Florida's.

LEACH: Tremendous game. It ended up being an underappreciated Indiana team at that time.

PRATT: When we played them a second time, we were in control of the game. Not the whole way but definitely in the second half. You never felt comfortable up there in that game at Bloomington. We had a couple of guys got into foul trouble. We might be ahead by two or three points, but we couldn't put any distance, or they couldn't put any distance between us and them. It was a tight ballgame and the place was going nuts. It was a terrific atmosphere. The tension, the excitement—nobody could pull away. It was nip and tuck and that even got the fans more fired up. The rivalry and the sellout. The second game was played on a neutral floor and it was not the same.

LEACH: The next big game was Louisville, but I can't remember much of significance about that one. Russ Smith had 30. Michael Kidd-Gilchrist had 24 points, 19 rebounds. He was just a force in that game. He took the most shots, got to the line 13 times, didn't have a single turnover. He was the guy, if there was a big game, you'd want him on your team.

PRATT: When he scored big. He worked the glass and found a way to be fouled while he was shooting on some putbacks or even low post offense for him. He could draw the foul, get to the foul line when he was playing at his best.

LEACH: I guess the officials were worried about the rivalry because it seemed to be one of those games that was over-officiated. Over 50 fouls called in the game.

PRATT: That was a stretch where Louisville was upset with Cousins and that group from 2010. The rivalry had heated up. And of course that's when Calipari came to Kentucky in '10, and that was a situation where a couple of guys got tangled up and tempers flared and from that point on, as long as Pitino was there, there was always some kind of crisis or some kind of background stuff. He said this, he said that. And Pitino walked off the floor and flipped the bird at the fans [a few years later], and that didn't help quiet the rivalry.

LEACH: The regular season played out and they chugged along with very little trouble. They were down six at the half at Tennessee and ended up winning by three. The other thing I remember, as it got into February, you would just see from week to week how Anthony would add something. Catching lobs and blocking shots at the start of the year, and he was growing as a player and adding so much more to his game each week.

PRATT: Cal let him go to the short corner and then he went to the elbow for jump shots, catch and shoot, and he got really confident with that. I don't know if he ever took a three that year but remember, he was just a post-up guy to start. Paint guy. He went to the short corner for the "J," went to the elbow. Really grew his game offensively. One thing I remember about that year: Vanderbilt had a good team, always tough for Kentucky to play down there. The game in Nashville was an eight-point game and at Rupp it was a nine-point game, so then they end up facing Vanderbilt for the championship. They had Jenkins and that crew then. He was a sharpshooter. Then Vanderbilt upsets them by six, seven points in the championship game of the SEC, and everybody was all worried about how it might affect the tournament. Kentucky had only one loss until then and everybody said, "Oh, no, they've lost their mojo; this will hurt their confidence going to the NCAA," but it was just one of those things—you play a team three times in a season, sometimes the matchups don't work out for you like they usually do. Down there in New Orleans, that championship game in the Superdome, Kentucky just didn't match up good that game and took the "l."

LEACH: That was the game that Cal told the story that Michael came to him to suggest that Darius get to start because he'd been struggling a little bit. He ended up leading them in scoring 16, so it seemed to have served its purpose in that regard because Darius became a big factor in the NCAA run.

PRATT: Darius gets overlooked a lot. He was a four-year guy and you watched him develop, gain confidence. He lost a lot of confidence when Billy Clyde was at Kentucky. Sometimes he had an up and down confidence with Cal, but what's interesting about that team, they had two glue guys, Michael Kidd Gilchrest and Darius Miller, I thought.

LEACH: Darius more quietly.

PRATT: Yes, Darius more quietly and a better perimeter shooter. He could knock down that corner shot. He wasn't afraid to take the shot. They are two different players but boy, they did all the dirty work.

LEACH: Darius—the year before, they lost a game by two down at Ole Miss—and Darius turned down a potential game-winning shot and Cal got down on him for doing that, but to Darius's credit and to Cal's too, he came back to gain Cal's trust again for those kinds of shots, and he became a real strong influence in their title run the next year.

PRATT: He came off the bench. A kid who grew up in Kentucky and won a state championship. I think his time at Kentucky meant more than most guys because he was a Kentuckian and he spent four years there. He brought the juice when he came off the bench.

LEACH: When they got in the NCAA tournament, they handled the two games there in Louisville pretty easily. I thought the game with Indiana was tougher than the one with Baylor of the two in Atlanta. What about you?

PRATT: Yeah. I think it had more emotion, so it made it tougher after the way the other game ended [in Bloomington] and the rivalry. Maybe Baylor seemed like a bit of a letdown. People thought of Baylor as a football school. We just played Indiana and we got our revenge. You know how that thinking goes. I was a little bit concerned because Baylor was really athletic and played hard. After that IU game we ran out of juice in that game, emotionally and physically, but Kentucky took it. Baylor got after you, man.

They were ranked higher than IU, ninth in the country in the last poll. They would come at you full court and they just climbed the boards. They just tried to beat you up.

LEACH: Terrence Jones had his best game of the tournament against Baylor. The thing about that team was that different guys could lead the way on a given night. Lamb had a big game in the final, AD in the semifinal, and Teague led them in scoring against Iowa State in the second round. So it was on to New Orleans, and for all the hype about the Duke/Carolina rivalry, they've never met in the NCAA Tournament. So now you've got Kentucky versus Louisville in a Final Four. What do you remember about the lead-up to that game?

PRATT: There was a lot of yapping from fans. That's natural. Both sides. The fans really got into it. Our hotel was right there off of Bourbon Street and I remember seeing some of the players walking around even with the U of L guys. They knew each other through AAU so it wasn't as bitter or as hostile as the fans made it out to be. I remember standing on the corner, taking the crowd in, watching the people, and here comes a couple of our guys and a couple of their guys walking down the street together, and they've got their stuff on so you know who they are—plus they're so tall. They were having a good time. They were really enjoying the Final Four. This wasn't game day; it was the day before, but then you'd look around and the fans wanted to fight. They'd fuss and holler at each other. [laughter] And these kids are just walking through the French Quarter with each other.

LEACH: Anthony was just sensational. He dominated the boards. They threw a lob up and it seemed like he reached back farther than is humanly possible to catch a bad pass and dunk it. And it was on that stage where he was already recognized as the Player of the Year. You saw what was to come in the NBA when he got onto that stage in the Final Four.

PRATT: And I remember two things. One, you and I walked over to a different hotel where they made one of the presentations about AD being Player of the Year. His mom and dad were there, and what struck me was they weren't very tall. [*laughter*] When they were introduced, I thought, "How did they have a seven-footer? "

LEACH: The thing I remember about the U of L game, Kentucky only made two threes, but Darius hit a big one. Louisville had made a little bit of a run, their last run, and Darius killed it off with a big three. That was interesting in the context of what I was talking about earlier and that shot he turned down at Ole Miss.

PRATT: They were so strong on the glass with Darius, Kidd-Gilchrist and Jones and AD. They didn't need the three. They had too much inside all the way around. AD didn't take that many shots. It was Jones and Kidd-Gilchrist, putbacks from Darius. That's pretty amazing that you win a game, won the semifinals, with only taking seven treys and making two.

LEACH: And then they get to the finals and play Kansas. I was pretty confident they were going to win. I thought it was Kentucky or Carolina. You also liked Louisville. Anybody that gets to the national championship game is good enough to beat you, but I was going to be surprised if Kentucky didn't win it. I think one thing that kept it close was Anthony couldn't make a shot. Cal tells the story about what he said at halftime, but Doron had a huge game [22 points]. I remember talking to someone after their shootaround because in those days we weren't allowed to attend them, and I was told that Doron was lighting it up and it certainly carried over to the game.

PRATT: Louisville scared me the most because our first game with them was a really good ballgame. A six-point game. I thought they had the right balance and I thought a guy gets hot in the Final Four because the game tightens up, it gets shorter and if a guy's having a big game, just unconscious like Russ Smith could get, the game could get away from you. That first game was much tougher for us than the Kansas game. The first time we played Kansas I thought for most of the game we were in control. They had the big bruiser inside. He tried to take it at AD all the time. Thomas Robinson. AD wouldn't let him get into his body, and part of that game was they wanted Robinson to get into AD's body, get him in foul trouble, and Robinson was a lot bigger as far as bulk than AD—but he couldn't do it. He couldn't get in there and draw those fouls. So I thought we really played for the championship against Louisville.

LEACH: In the final game, as the seconds are ticking down, when you're in this kind of job that you and I are in at a place like Kentucky, you figure you're gonna get to a few Final Fours and there's a decent chance you're going to get to call a championship and get in the club with Cawood and Ralph and the rest, so it was fun when that finally happened.

PRATT: It was. That was a fun team to watch. All three of Cal's first teams were different, but they all were fun to watch. I enjoyed Brandon Knight the year before and this year, you just had a lot of talent. We were spoiled as far as the talent we got to watch. When you play your whole year and you lose your second game in the conference tournament, you gotta be riding high and you don't worry about a whole lot of things. As long as you had the big eraser back there in AD you were in good shape. And again, I tell you what, Marquis Teague, Calipari got him to change his whole approach to the game and decide he's going to facilitate for others first and put himself second. That happened sometime late December, early January. That's hard to do—give Calipari and Teague a lot of credit for doing that.

LEACH: We'll close on this. We ought to mention Terrence; we haven't mentioned him much. Here was a guy who came out with as big a high school rep as anybody and he didn't push to be the superstar of the team. He gave space to Anthony and others and just did his job, played the role Calipari needed him to play rather than worry about getting his points.

PRATT: Because of that, everyone was concerned whether he could be the guy next year that they thought he could be and lead the team in scoring and everything else. The way he handled that year was totally different. He averaged 12 a game that year. So Terrance blended right in and accepted his role and that might have been the key to the whole team. Accepting their role. It was a really good defensive team, anchored by AD. The other thing that jumps out at me is that on a given day they all could score the ball and they could score it from different positions on the floor. Jones could post. He had a nice little midrange game. Darius could move out and shoot the three, then Teague, when they backed off him, he could get to the charity stripe, with those elbows could make it tough on people, so offensively that was a really good team and a good defensive team too, but you become a good defensive team because you could push out, you could really hound a guy who's got the ball or try to deny a position because you've got the big fella, you've got the eraser back there. That made our defense a lot better. He didn't have the same effect on offense, did he? He didn't get many shots and he didn't care.

LEACH: I know you take pride in taking a professional approach to this job. Cawood always told me it's okay if the fans know you want Kentucky to win if you're the University of Kentucky announcer, but you should still strive to paint an accurate picture of what is happening. I know you approach it that way, as Jeff Piecoro does [and Jeff Van Note before him in my tenure] in football. With all of that said, it still had to be special to be sitting there at courtside to see a national championship won by the program that you gave your blood, sweat, and tears to over a four-year period, right?

PRATT: I'm usually pretty happy if UK wins and a little bummed out if they lose. I try to go into it with an open mind, like when I'm scouting a team, but when you win a national championship, you're certainly very proud of them. That's why it's more difficult to take a neutral position. You want to talk about the game in a positive manner for both teams. You have a little bit of a former player look, a little bit of a former coach look, and then sometimes I just enjoy being a spectator. I get a lot of texts [from former players and teammates] all the time, whether we're doing good or bad. It's fun to get other people's thoughts on what you're looking at.

LEACH: I don't have that former player perspective. My view came from growing up listening to Cawood and Ralph call so many Kentucky games. Anybody who is fortunate enough to have this job figures they will probably get to call a national championship if they stay in the job long enough, so I remember thinking it was fun and a great honor to join that club. And I got a text from Ralph about that very fact, which I really appreciated. He was the only one left at that point that knew that feeling, as a UK play-by-play announcer. And TJ Beisner, now with our UK Network team, happened to snap a picture of me doing the postgame radio interview with Cal on the court with confetti streaming down. Cal and I have laughed about how much younger we both look.

2013

Nerlens Noel and Willie Cauley-Stein are the players from this team who had long runs in the NBA. Cauley-Stein was still very raw at this point, so in retrospect, it was a team that didn't have the overall talent of Calipari's first three squads. The guard play was inconsistent for this team, and when Noel went down with a season-ending injury, the season was essentially over—and this was probably a club that would have done well to get to the Sweet 16 even with Noel still in the lineup. Still, the season did produce a few memorable moments, including one in the opening game.

LEACH: The first noteworthy moment of this season came in the first game, up in Brooklyn. May have been the first game played in that Barclays Center. They went up there and played what we thought was a good Maryland team. Jarrod Polson was the star of the game. Good example of a guy who comes as a walk-on, Kentucky kid who probably comes in with the expectation he may not play much but is good enough to play. He got his chance and came through, so he ended up being a role player for the next two years. Great example of a guy seizing the only opportunity he might get.

PRATT: That was a perfect storm for Jarrod. I remember everybody going, "Wow, we won it with a walk-on."

LEACH: He showed he could play so Cal came to trust him.

PRATT: He showed Cal some toughness too. Cal likes that.

LEACH: The other game I remember most was the Senior Day

game against Florida. Julius Mays hit the clinching free throws and brought his little girl out with him and it was a touching scene, and Cal had challenged the fans to stand up for the last part of the game and they did. So in a bad season that was a nice moment but a clunker performance in the SEC Tournament, and the NIT first-round loss at Robert Morris left a bad taste in the fans' mouths. Mays was Cal's first grad transfer. At that time, Calipari was very much against that path to get players because of how it would impact mid-major coaches but, as we have seen, the landscape of the sport has changed markedly on that front.

PRATT: The transfer thing and adapting to it is similar to adapting to the three-point shot and adapting to dealing with AAU coaches in recruiting. Those changes were major, not like a jump ball or how many timeouts you get. These are changes that really affected college basketball. Julius was a tough guy and I remember the chatter was like, "I'm not sure if he's good enough," and he stepped in there, played hard, and was a good defender. He was an excellent pickup. He wasn't a ball-dominant guard like Archie Goodwin, but he could hit the open shot. I thought he had a heckuva year.

LEACH: The buzz from that Maryland game faded a few days later when they lost at Duke, but it was when they lost up at Notre Dame to a pretty average Notre Dame team that I started to have some serious doubts about how good they would be. Then they lost at home to Baylor—Calipari's first loss in Rupp as UK coach.

PRATT: The Duke game down in Atlanta, Alex Poythress had a big game and everybody was fired up about him. He was our best player down there. He was powerful; he got out in transition. He shot the ball. Then he struggled from then on.

LEACH: They lost to Louisville, who was ranked fourth, and ended up winning the national championship and Archie had one of his best games. He and Ryan Harrow combined for 39 points in what was probably one of the Cats' best performances of that season.

PRATT: Archie was on fire and he carried us. Never saw a shot he didn't like. He was really good in that game. Those two guys lit it up and Pitino was playing a lot of zone.

LEACH: So they go into conference play, three games after the Louisville game, Elston Turner Jr. came in and scored 40 against them and Texas A&M hung another Rupp loss on them.

PRATT: Turner Jr. did everything he could to get points and got them. It was embarrassing. But they went down to Aggieland and won that game in overtime in the rematch.

LEACH: He was seven of 23 in the next game. Usually Cal's teams, you're not gonna beat them the same way twice. So they found a way to defend Turner. Beat South Carolina by 22, beat Auburn by 10 in Lexington. Then they go to Florida and Noel gets hurt in the second half of that game, and the Gators were good but Kentucky would have certainly played in the tournament that year had Nerlens not gotten hurt. That was really the end of the season other than that Florida win. Tennessee beat them by 30 and Kentucky lost six of its last 10 games. But even with Nerlens, that team wasn't going very far. Kinda like the 2021 season, it was a struggle at the point guard position. Ryan Harrow could certainly score, as he would later demonstrate at Georgia State in a fine career there, but he struggled in that point guard, as well as the spotlight that is on Kentucky players.

PRATT: He was a streaky shooter. He could get going, but the league he played in with Georgia State, it's not the same league physically. The SEC, outside of the Big Ten, it's a very physical league. I'm not gonna use the word *shock,* but it was different for him. Not used to being bumped and hit. You know, for the most part the ACC has been a finesse league.

LEACH: Ryan came from NC State so that's a good point. A shock to his system.

PRATT: The other thing about him, he couldn't beat a lot of people off the bounce. Now Archie could and he would. He put up some shots that you thought, "What the hell?" [*laughter*]

LEACH: Just a quick thought about the NIT game up at Robert Morris. Having seen them play so flat against Vandy in the SEC Tournament, it just kind of felt like everybody was ready for the season to be over. They'd missed any chance at the NCAA tournament. The Sweet 16 was being played in Lexington so they had to go play on Robert Morris's home floor even though Kentucky should have had the home game. So that's a big deal for Robert Morris and when we got there, their students were lined up waiting to get in and it was a huge deal for them to have the University of Kentucky basketball team coming into that building. Jimmy Dykes and maybe Brad Nessler were doing the game for ESPN, and I went over to Jimmy before the game because their spot and our spot were right there in front of the student section and I said, "We both realize what might happen tonight so it's every man for himself when this is over," and he laughed. But I wasn't surprised that Robert Morris would win the game because for the Kentucky guys, when they lost to Vanderbilt and lost any chance at the NCAA tournament, I think everybody was ready for the season to be over.

PRATT: I agree. The body language was not good up there. Robert Morris played a lot of zone if I remember right, and we struggled to make shots.

LEACH: Two for 10 on threes. They were 19 of 30 on twos but couldn't make a three and missed some free throws. Kyle Wiltjer had a three from the wing in front of us that would have won it but didn't go. Then all of the students naturally rushed the floor. They did it in a manner in which we were not threatened to be overrun. Disappointing end to a season after that Florida game kind of gave you a little hope. That loss to Vandy kinda broke their spirit.

PRATT: What were Willie's numbers that year?

LEACH: He was a freshman, scored 242 points in 29 games, so about nine points a game. He shot about 62 percent from the field, blocked 60 shots. Had 48 turnovers. Willie shot 37 percent at the free-throw line. He came back and by the 2015 season had worked at it and was a 62 percent free-throw shooter so it was not his strongest suit, but he clearly worked at it and got better, to his credit. That first year, however, you thought he was avoiding getting fouled because he didn't want to go to the line.

PRATT: They didn't play him late either. If Nerlens doesn't get hurt, then you don't worry about not having Willie in there late, but you need somebody in there for the defensive side of it and to block the shot, which Willie could really do, but they had to play him and he was shooting and he did not want to go to that charity stripe. That recruiting class. It was Goodwin, Poythress, two guys highly thought of, Nerlens highly thought of. Willie was the guy they said, "Well, he's a good athlete so we'll turn him into something." He was rough around the edges when he got there and the problem was Nerlens wasn't much of an offensive threat but he could block shots and rebound and he was further along in his development than Willie, so when Nerlens goes down, we have to play Willie a lot of minutes and that just didn't work out.

Jim Barnhart (producer/engineer), Mike, and Tom at UCLA's Pauley Pavilion (December 2015)

Jim Host with Tom at Lahaina Civic Center, Maui (November 2005)

Jim Barnhart, Tom, and Mike at Rupp Arena (March 2021)

Jim Barnhart, Tom, and Mike in a remote broadcast studio at Memorial Coliseum (February 2021)

Mike, Tom, Jim Barnhart, and Matt Jones during a preseason broadcast at Isaacs National Gymnasium, Nassau, Bahamas (July 2014)

Christmas lunch at Ramsey's Restaurant, Lexington, with current and past UK Radio Network crew members: Mike Dodson, Kyle Macy, Tom, Ralph Hacker, John Short, Oscar Combs, and Tom Devine (December 2017)

Tom with James Lee of the 1978 UK national title team, Rupp Arena (February 2018)

Mike at the replica of the White House pressroom podium,
George H. W. Bush Library, Texas A&M University (February
2020)

The UK Network broadcast crew in the 1996 Final Four ties: Mike Dodson, Mike Pratt, Oscar Combs, Matt Jones, Jim Barnhart, and Tom Leach

Former Voice of the Wildcats Ralph Hacker, Tom, and Mike at Rupp Arena (November 2019)

UK Hall of Famers Chuck Hayes and Mike at Vandy's Memorial Gymnasium during a UK practice (January 2020)

Tom with UK Hall of Famer Jack "Goose" Givens at a golf outing (2013)

Former Voice of the Wildcats Ralph Hacker, Jim Barnhart, Mike, Tom, and Oscar Combs at Jim Host's house (July 2016)

Tom and Mike hitch a ride on Dr. Pease Lyons's private plane to get home sooner after the win over Wichita State in the NCAA Tournament (March 2014)

Mike, Tom, and Jim Barnhart courtside at the ballroom in the Atlantis, Nassau, where Kentucky played exhibition games (August 2018)

Tom and Mike courtside at Rupp Arena (early 2000s) (photo courtesy of Victoria Graff)

Jim Barnhart, Tom, and Mike courtside at Rupp (2013) (photo courtesy of Victoria Graff)

2014

With what the Cats had accomplished in Calipari's first three years, there was very little discontentment expressed about how 2013 played out, especially given the hype surrounding the arrival of another top-ranked recruiting class, which included Julius Randle and the twins Andrew and Aaron Harrison. Nonetheless, it was ridiculous that some hoped for an undefeated season for that group since six of the top eight players were freshmen. But those expectations heightened the disappointment that followed from some close losses spread throughout the season, and then some panic started to show among fans when UK took back-to-back losses to average Arkansas and South Carolina teams. But this team found itself at the SEC Tournament, with the famous "tweak" from Cal, and what followed was a truly incredible run to the national title game.

LEACH: Kentucky had three really good runs, a bad year in '13, and they come back with a number one recruiting class and everybody just thinks they're instantly gonna bounce back and be what they were in 2010, 2011, and 2012, but those teams all had a little more experience than the '14 team, and a lot of that fell on Andrew and Aaron. There was so much hype around that recruiting class and the twins ended up catching a little more heat than was justified.

PRATT: They came in with big reputations and what they were was solid basketball players, high IQ. Athletically, Andrew was not as good an athlete as Aaron, but he was a very good leader, an excellent point guard. He knew how to use his body and get to the paint and create for other people.

LEACH: Yeah, getting him to do more creating for his teammates was all the famous "tweak" by Calipari amounted to. And I also think all the attention that was focused on the twins caused Julius Randle to get a little overlooked on just how good his one season was. He had 24 games with double figures in points and rebounds. Issel's final season with 25 was the only one better—and that to me is a very underappreciated stat.

PRATT: He was a power player who could get to the foul line. With Willie struggling from the charity stripe and not wanting to go there, Randle loved to go there. He was all about getting fouled and putting the ball in the basket. He was that inside threat. He was a heck of a rebounder. If you look at his stats getting to the charity stripe, he was by far the leader of that team and man, he could score, get to the foul line and rebound. I thought this team was pretty well put together as far as inside out. You had Randle inside, very powerful. Willie could rebound and do a few things and Young was a shooter. He's another one who never saw a shot he didn't like. Aaron could shoot it and Andrew; the twins took a beating publicly, via social media, but they were really good college players.

LEACH: That team is remembered as one that was mediocre until the postseason, but they were a little better than that. Florida beat them by 19 in the last game of the regular season but nobody else blew them out. It's just, losing four of the last seven and coming on the heels of 2013's NIT year, that team got really beat up by the critics.

PRATT: You make a good point. Florida was number one at the time. They ended up in the Final Four with us, not against us but with us. So the Cats got butchered down there and I remember everybody just throwing in the towel around the city and the fans. You can't get beaten that bad, even though they were number one, but then they turn around and played Florida really tough in the finals of the SEC Tournament. James Young was going for the last shot to win it and I thought he had the guy beat. I don't think he got fouled—he just slipped in the paint and lost the ball. We might have won that game.

LEACH: The first two times they played Florida, sometimes you have a team that the matchup—you could play them 100 times and you'd lose 98 or 99 of them. It's not a good matchup. I had the feeling that that Kentucky team against a really good veteran Florida team, that they could play them 100 times and would lose most of them, but when they did what nearly beat the Gators, I think that loss gave them a lot of confidence.

PRATT: They won two in a row [in the tournament] and should have won three in a row, so that made them feel pretty good.

LEACH: In the NCAA Tournament, they beat Kansas State in St. Louis and coming into the Wichita State game—this goes back to when they played Ohio State in 2011—my sense was that the coaches thought they had the guys in a really good place mentally with their confidence. They thought they had a real shot against Wichita State, which was undefeated and legit good.

PRATT: The Kansas State game I thought they didn't play as well as they had been playing in the SEC Tournament. It was a struggle. Kansas State played a lot of zone, in and out of the zone and Kentucky kind of shot poorly. They had played so well in the SEC Tournament and should have won the damn thing. All of a sudden, they're playing back to where they were during the season sometimes. But boy, that Wichita State game, that was a classic. The intensity level was significantly better than Kansas State. Wichita State thought they could go undefeated that year and they played their ass off, and that little Fred VanFleet guy who goes to the G-League and now he's a starter with Toronto. He was a tough dude and he ran the show for them.

LEACH: He played 35 minutes, had one turnover, Cleanthony Early and Ron Baker, I thought one of those guys would be nice pros and it turned out VanFleet ended up being the best pro. Early had 31, Baker had 20; those were two really good college players.

PRATT: They were a heck of a team, they could rebound. That was a Final Four–type game.

LEACH: Absolutely. Kentucky played at a high level. Shot over 50 percent , only 11 turnovers, out-rebounded Wichita State by nine. Cats only missed 23 shots and they got 10 of them back. So that speaks to the passion and the effort that it was going to take to beat a team as good as Wichita State, and Kentucky was able to bring that.

PRATT: And all the controversy throughout the year about how Kentucky was playing faded away quickly. They had experienced the ups and downs of the year and expectations of the people who felt like they didn't live up to. I remember watching shootaround when it was open, then watching the guys as they warmed up— they thought they could beat the NBA champions at that point.

LEACH: Next up was another upset, over Louisville, and I'm looking at the box score from that game: Dominique Hawkins played 15 minutes, and the only thing, all the way across in his stat line is three personal fouls. He didn't take a shot, didn't get a steal, nothing. Everything is zero except three fouls, but he played 15 minutes and his contribution was huge. They lost Willie, their best defender, to an injury early in that game, and Dom got in Russ Smith's head. Smith got 23 points, but it took him 20 shots to get there. And Poythress plays 14 minutes and gives them six points. He played big off the bench. Then they had another unexpected hero in the next game against Michigan with Marcus Lee.

PRATT: He had some big blocks and some putback dunks. He had a hell of a game.

LEACH: So we're off to Dallas for the Final Four, to play Wisconsin. I remember talking to a friend of mine, J. C. Faulkner, a friend from grade school who is a huge Cat fan. He called to talk about the matchup, and I said, "The way Kentucky is playing right now, I like their chances, and the only way I think they lose is if Wisconsin outscores them something like 10-2 on threes." Well, it ended up being 8-2, and if it had been 10-2, Kentucky would have lost. The other thing I remember, Aaron hit the shot and it was right there in front of us in our broadcast spot [we were by the free-throw line]. Andrew kicked it out to Aaron and he kind of looked at it for a second, and it was three to go ahead or two to tie so they had to respect the drive as well, and he went up and hit the shot and then Wisconsin goes down and misses, and I remember Aaron jumped off that elevated court and right behind us were his mom and dad. He went to hug his mom. That was a neat moment to see. He was on that incredible run.

My old high school made it to the Sweet 16 in 1984—it was a similar to this Kentucky season 30 years later. Bourbon County had a team in the region, Clark County, they could have played 100 times and never have beaten. Clark County got upset by Maysville so Bourbon County didn't have to face them so Bourbon County ends up winning the tournament, gets to the state tournament, and they had this kid named Jeff Royce that hit three last-second shots to get them to the state finals. When people ask me about Aaron Harris, I remember that weekend. People would say, "Have you ever seen anything like that?" and I would say, "Yes, one time." That's a clutch shooter to do that three games in a row and then the Wichita State game, they hit big shots.

PRATT: At that point in time, they were so confident, they'd gone from people questioning them during the regular season to all of a sudden you're now playing as you'd hoped to play, the way other people expected you to play. I remember calling Jimmy O'Brien, who I played with on the Colonels one year, and he coached Ohio

State and I wanted a scouting report on Wisconsin. I asked him, "Will they play any zone?" and he said, "They'll put Bo in his coffin before he plays the zone." It was so true. They had size. They were not the fastest or the quickest, but they were strong and went to the glass.

LEACH: That gets them to the championship game against UConn. At that point, with UConn having upset Florida, I think the feeling among the Kentucky fans and the people who covered Kentucky in the media was that everything had fallen into place for them and they were going to get this very unlikely championship. I sure felt that way, but as it turned out, they might have been better off playing Florida, as good as Florida was, just because they knew them so well. This is one thing where I thought not having Willie hurt them a little bit, with those two guards from UConn, they ended up being 13 of 22, Ryan Boatright and Shabazz Napier, Napier in particular; they were small, quick guards, they were hard for our guys to guard, but Willie could have switched off on them.

PRATT: Your point is well taken because one of the reasons Willie is still playing is because he can block shots and guard out on the perimeter, and a lot of the bigs cannot handle the pick and roll as far as when the ball comes over the pick. Big guys get beat all the time by the smaller, quicker guys. So Willie, he would stretch out, he wasn't gonna give up anything. He could have contained those guys in ball screen situations. He's still very good at that. It's one of his real pluses in the NBA.

LEACH: Somewhere in the second half Alex got a bad call, a charging foul where he was going to score to either tie it up or take the lead, and he got called for charging. UConn went down and hit a big shot, it was early in the second half, and I thought this just doesn't feel good. These games seem to be going a certain way and sometimes you just kind of get a sense the matchup is not working or something isn't right for your team to have its best chance of winning. So early in the second half, the game didn't have a good feel to it for Kentucky to have a shot to win it.

PRATT: I felt that way at halftime because you're in the national championship and the second half, it's not a 20-minute game, it's more like a 14-minute game, and we were down four points at halftime. Four is not a lot but people tighten up. Players, coaches tighten up. The game clock shortens because people are playing conservatively. They don't want to make a mistake. This is the last 20 minutes of basketball for the year, so playing from behind is extremely tough in a situation like that. And Coach Jim Calhoun threw some zone in there too, I think, and that kind of slowed us down at times. You're more hesitant and you're already tight because you're playing for the national championship. That was a heartbreaker.

LEACH: To be in that spot was very much unexpected, and then when Florida got upset on the other side, it felt like things were falling into place, but those two guards were just a tough matchup for Kentucky. They were small and quick and were playing with a lot of confidence because of the run they had gotten on. They had beaten good teams and so they were riding high as well.

PRATT: To experience working a Final Four and then experience winning one, and all the excitement when people go crazy and all that confetti dropped down from the air. We watched it as a winner and then as a loser and man, it was a totally different feeling. It is really cool when you win it all—the vibe when you win it all.

2015

All that crazy "going undefeated" talk of the previous summer was missing going into this season, but it would have been justified for this season—and it nearly happened. The recruiting class wasn't as highly touted as some others, but it turned out to be just as good. Karl-Anthony Towns became the best big man in the country, and you'd have go to a long way back to find four guards as good as the Harrison twins plus Tyler Ulis and Devin Booker. Wisconsin spoiled the party at the Final Four but when this team was at its best, it was far and away the best team in the country.

LEACH: This season started in the Bahamas with a set of six exhibition games. I remember the first practice in that high school gym where they played, and before they could start, they had to get the rim adjusted. It was a little too high or low—can't remember which—but I just recall John Robic kneeling beneath the basket with a tape measure and Cal on the ladder at the rim and it looked like that scene from *Hoosiers.* When the games started, there were some jaw-dropping moments with incredible dunks, and when you saw Ulis and Hawkins completely suffocating opposing backcourts and realizing they couldn't even crack the starting lineup, you started to realize how good this team could be.

PRATT: When we saw them play down there in the Bahamas, I was really impressed. Trey Lyles and Willie Cauley-Stein didn't even play—they were both injured. I'm watching those games and thinking, "Damn, this team is really good without those guys, so where are those guys going to get their minutes?" That's a good problem to have. Three guys back from the Final Four team: the Harrisons and Willie. So the guards had good experience but outside of that, we didn't really know. At that point, you didn't know about Booker, didn't know about Karl Anthony-Towns. They both were freshmen. You had Ulis there. He was a freshman and he came back the next year. But look at that schedule. We beat six ranked teams by an average of 17 points that year.

LEACH: Once the season started, that 72-40 rout of Kansas in the Champions Classic kinda took your breath away.

PRATT: That was a shocker, the way we handled that game. There was another game that I thought was quite interesting. When we played Texas, they were ranked sixth. We handled them pretty well. Then we played at Louisville [a few weeks later]. They were ranked four and we were one. Whenever you get a matchup like that, there's typically not a big gap between the two. Louisville played that thing down to the wire. It was 58-50. I think beating Louisville at Louisville and winning those two overtime games that followed, I think just shot this team through the rest of the league play. Surviving a couple of scares and beating a quality team like Louisville on the road. As a player, if you can win games like that, you think, "Damn, we're rolling now. I'm playing pretty good," or however you want to put it.

LEACH: Yes, they had a couple of scares when conference play started. Should have probably lost to Ole Miss if Stefan Moody had not cramped up. Then there was a two-overtime game down at Texas A&M. This question came up later in the year when the streak got up to about 30 games—is it good to have a loss before the tournament rather than go in undefeated and have all of that pressure? What were your thoughts on that particular debate for that team?

PRATT: I don't believe in taking a loss to help yourself in the next games. You play to win, and you play to get better every time. That, to me, is the ultimate goal. Calipari doesn't like to talk about winning. He likes to talk about getting better every game. And that's true, but you always want to win no matter how many in a row. Just keep winning because confidence comes with continued wins. You want to be pushed and to have to win a couple of tough games. Figure out who your go-to guys are. Who you can count on? What kind of plays are going to be successful? You need some tight games where your team can react. Now, do you have to lose some of those to get better? No. You have to win those by doing what you are coached to do. You do those things, you win the games, players look at you like you're a genius and they feel good about themselves too because they did what they were trained to do.

LEACH: We talked about Anthony Davis in 2012 and how he developed as the season went along. It's probably worth talking about Karl because in the first half or so of the year, somewhere in conference play, it started to turn for him. He'd float outside on the perimeter and shoot a few threes but at some point, I think Cal and with Assistant Coach Kenny Payne basically said, "Big fella, we need you down low and it's in your own best interest to play down in that block." Karl did what they wanted him to do, as he was very coachable, and then he took off and blew by Okafor at Duke as the best player in the country.

PRATT: He exerted his will on people instead of just kind of floating around and taking whatever came his way. He decided he was going to force himself on the opposition and see if they could stop him—and they couldn't stop him, so he gained confidence. He believed he could affect the outcome of the game and he did.

LEACH: Late in the year, next-to-last game, playing in Georgia, and you've got this streak going and they had to make clutch plays, and they made them. I remember Shannon Spake came to be, like, the Kentucky reporter because she was doing the TV sideline reporting for so many of the Kentucky games. So she's in Georgia doing her regular gig but they also send Jeanine Edwards to do a sidebar story for SportsCenter, and I remember being at shootaround and seeing all of this and thinking, "This is really starting to get big because ESPN has gone to the expense of sending in another crew to do stories on Kentucky."

PRATT: I always said the media circus, it was like we were in a big tent and everybody was under it—the media, the players, the coaches—and it was a traveling circus. We saw all of this stuff develop. There were more people around, bigger press conferences, and you could just sense that something was going on. These kids are getting the same questions over and over and over. That could have worn you down, but it did not wear those guys down. Every stop along the way it seemed like the crowd under the tent got bigger. That was tough for those kids.

Getting back to the team, I mentioned the three players back and the Harrison twins at guard, you can talk about Karl a lot. He was terrific. He really became a quality player, but I think it was the development and the growth of the Harrisons—in particular Andrew—who really figured out how to control the team, how to get out of the team what Cal wanted. I think they got connected the year before in that Final Four run and they kept it up. He was a solid athlete but not a great athlete, but Ulis comes off the bench and picks up the vibe about what Calipari wanted. He added a whole other dimension to the athletic guard spot. So you've got Andrew Harrison, who is in sync with Calipari, they're really playing well, then you come off the bench with the little guy [Ulis], and he's shaking everybody up with his speed and quickness and getting things done like Calipari wanted. It goes back to what we said about this [2021] team—we didn't have a point guard to do those things.

LEACH: As we go through the postseason, not much to talk about until the Notre Dame game. I didn't foresee the trouble Notre Dame gave them, and it took everything they had to survive. I thought it was a case of how well Notre Dame played more than anything Kentucky did not do, and basically Karl was unstoppable and that is what avoided the upset. Andrew played really well at the end too.

PRATT: West Virginia was supposed to be the team that snuck up on us because they were physical and a top 20 team, but we beat them handily. We met that challenge of the physicality and then Notre Dame had a bunch of shooters. They got to the corners and they'd nail a three-point shot or just nail a shot. They played in a very deliberate—not slow but a deliberate—pace. They wanted to do certain things offensively. The last thing they wanted was to run and shoot with Kentucky, but if they could dictate the tempo, they felt that their shooting could keep them in the ballgame.

LEACH: They had a good plan and executed it well.

PRATT: I remember Willie Cauley-Stein made a play that was one of the best I've ever seen in a college game.

LEACH: Where he ran the length of the floor with Grant on the last shot?

PRATT: That was spectacular. Grant was probably going to make that shot, but Willie tracked him all the way down and blocked that shot and didn't foul, and Willie was flying and Grant was flying so the opportunity to try to block a shot and foul was pretty high when guys are going that fast. That was an amazing play. Give the man credit.

LEACH: So it was on to the Final Four in Indianapolis. All along Wisconsin was the only team I didn't want to see them run into. Mainly because Wisconsin had a chip on their shoulder from the previous year when Kentucky had upset them to the Final Four, and when you get to the Final Four the games are hard enough because the teams are good, so you don't want any extra stuff, factors, variables to have to deal with. The other thing was, I don't think I gave enough credit to this, Wisconsin was about the only team in the country that was comparable to Kentucky in size. Alex got hurt early and was lost for the season and they had so much talent and depth that they were able to play just fine and not miss a beat, but I thought if a healthy Alex Poythress would have been playing all season that he might have been a nice option to have against Sam Dekker in that game.

PRATT: I think if you look at both teams, good defensive teams, and Kentucky played their smothering defense and the defensive keys were rebounding, shot blocking, and steals. So we had two big guys who could block shots, Karl and Willie. Very good rebounding team because they had overall size in that starting lineup but Wisconsin, they were like that too. They were a good defensive club. They could shoot the ball. They were strong like Kentucky was. Dekker and Frank Kaminsky, they were strong players, and they had Nigel Hayes, he was strong. Built a lot like Kentucky was built. I'm not sure they had as many shot blockers. Defensively, they were built like Kentucky. Both teams played with great intensity, so it was a terrific matchup.

LEACH: There were three times when Kentucky had shot clock violations and that would have been, if two of those three, if you just get a shot up on the board with that Kentucky team, there's a chance you get an offensive rebound. Even if you didn't score, if you could have used up another 30 seconds. They were so good at closing teams out that year. They were flawless in their execution and for whatever reason, Wisconsin did a nice job of forcing those shot clock violations and if Kentucky could have gotten shots up they might have been able to rebound one or two of them and used up more time, and using up the time would have been noteworthy whether you scored or not.

PRATT: Kentucky was really great late in ballgames. They had four guards: the Harrison twins, Ulis, Booker. Four really good foul shooters. If somebody got in foul trouble you might not have thought at that point in their careers that Ulis or Booker were as good as the twins, but they were sharp basketball guys who could shoot the fouls. You didn't really lose anything with those two guys off the bench. Again, we see this coming and it's all about guard play. That's where it all starts in the NCAA. Wisconsin had a really good, solid guards too.

LEACH: And they were experienced. They didn't make mistakes, and it seems like I remember you saying Wisconsin had a good plan for how they defended Willie, which helped them to defend Karl.

PRATT: Yeah. Nigel Hayes just planted himself in the lane. I go back to what my buddy Jimmy O'Brien told me about the coach [Bo Ryan] and Obie said they would put him in his grave before he plans a zone, but in essence, this kid would play in the paint [like a zone]. He didn't care where Willie went. As long as you didn't throw a lob, he could care less. He was in the paint looking to help out, particularly on Karl. They forced Karl off the block, facing the hoop as many times as they could. They didn't want him to play with his back to the basket. So if he put the ball on the floor or he got to the paint, there was Nigel Hayes. He didn't give a dang where Willie was. Let's be honest, Willie disappeared. He was supposed to be the best defensive player in the country; Kaminsky ate him up with something like 20 points and Willie just didn't have a very good game. Hayes just played in the middle of that paint and that really put an extra burden on Kentucky. I don't think they had seen much of that pressure on the ball.

LEACH: They had the size and bulk to do it.

PRATT: Yep, so then they're playing five on four and that's a pretty good advantage. I remember sitting courtside in that second half and I'm looking at Karl do a reverse pivot, facing the hoop, and he was looking for something and Wisconsin had reacted, Hayes is in the paint, the other guys are looking to give help. They know Karl can score. He's had a terrific second half of the season. So he's looking for someone to pass to and he's only got three other teammates and they're not where he wants them to be, which is the other side of the floor. Karl looked right at us because he kept looking to the other side of the floor. He'd been trained to look for that pass when the double team comes, or he thinks it's coming, and nobody's over there. Willie just went on the baseline and sat there. That wasn't of any help because he was right in the crowd that Wisconsin had created. In all honesty, it was a zone. They call it man to man but when they drop the kid into the paint who was guarding Willie it was, in essence, a zone, so you have got to skip the ball and he didn't have anybody to skip the ball to. I felt sorry for him because I'm looking right into his eyes and I know what he's thinking—"Man, there's space over there, why isn't anybody over there?" So it was well schemed defensively by Wisconsin.

LEACH: With Hayes playing that way and with Kaminsky being seven feet tall, were they able to be in a position to stay out on the shooters better than other teams had? So it made it harder to kick it out for a wide-open three? That size meant Wisconsin's perimeter defenders didn't have to leave their man because they had Kaminsky and Hayes to defend Karl.

PRATT: Yes. And they had Dekker, a six eight, six nine, very athletic player. They had some people who could do those things defensively. You're not going to beat Wisconsin at that point in time under Bo Ryan, off the bounce. He's going to take that away. You can get in some places but you're not going to, he's not going to let you just drive it to the rim. That's the way he plays defense. He's going to force you to make an extra pass, to move without the ball, to do those things to make his defense move. In the second half, we just bogged down the last 10 minutes. We kind of looked; we threw it to Karl. He looked; he threw it back out. Give Wisconsin credit.

LEACH: I think it's interesting too that the only two teams that were in a position to realistically make a run at doing what Indiana did in 1976, which was to go undefeated, were the UNLV team in '91 and Kentucky in '15, and both of them were beaten by a team that they knocked out of the Final Four the year before. Vegas had crushed Duke the year before and so Duke had a year to think about it plus a week to prepare, and you had the same thing here with Wisconsin, with the head coach, Bo Ryan, he's also thinking back to the good team he had in 2003 and he's not going to get there as often as Kentucky—have a shot getting there as often as Kentucky. Kentucky knocks him out in '03, Kentucky knocks him out in '14 when he was the higher seed, and so he and his players had a year to think about that and he and his staff had a week to prepare. That's why I was hoping the Cats would never see Wisconsin in that tournament.

PRATT: I agree. Last 10 minutes, we started laboring to get things done offensively. But they didn't tear us up at the other end. We did a nice job defensively too.

LEACH: Kentucky was struggling to score. I thought they tightened up a little bit. Maybe not, the players would only know, but it's human nature to think you're so close to something that is going to be and there's been so much buildup and you're in a position where you've closed out every one of those games all year long. Now, all of a sudden, the things you've done all year aren't working. In part, that's because you're facing the team best built to defend you, so you get a little tight.

PRATT: They were able to do to Kentucky what Kentucky had been doing to other teams, but it was a helluva game. Back and forth. Back and forth.

LEACH: When they got to the final, Wisconsin, their championship game was beating Kentucky. Playing Duke was a little anticlimactic. Whereas, for our guys, if they had beaten Wisconsin, I think they would have handled Duke, no problem.

PRATT: And to your point, I thought Wisconsin, after I left the game, I thought Wisconsin is going to win this thing. Then after I got home, I started thinking the day of the game, maybe it was such an emotional game against Kentucky that maybe there would be a bit of a letdown against Duke. Certainly, I think there was. Some coaches don't like to talk about revenge in the setting of playing a team that for whatever reason they've lost to eight times or had a controversial play, coaches don't like to talk about that a lot, but I'm going to tell you from the standpoint of the athlete, those things you don't forget. You do not forget those games. If you get beat by 30, you forget that game. What you don't forget, I can still see that shot that [Ohio State's Dave] Sorenson hit, banked in with no seconds on the clock to beat us to go to the Final Four [in 1968]. I still see it.

2016

Jamal Murray and Tyler Ulis formed as good a guard combo as Calipari had ever had, but there wasn't enough around them to merit the high ranking this team enjoyed when the season started. A convincing win over Duke in the Champions Classic fueled the hype train, but that Duke team ended up losing 11 games. Skal Labissiere wasn't comfortable playing with his back to the basket, so UK really had no low post presence, and that is one of the things that contributed to their season ending in the second round of the NCAA Tournament, against Indiana.

PRATT: The other thing with that team was that it was Isaiah Briscoe's first year and he really struggled. He was a freshman. He came in heralded and struggled to find a spot. They played him at the wing and sometimes at the point, but he struggled to generate offense consistently. I think they expected more than nine points a game out of him. Murray was a special shooter. Ulis, I didn't think he could ever generate 17 points a game offensively. I knew he could set his teammates up; he was really pesky on defense. He really had a high basketball IQ, but to think that he could go from coming off the bench the year before to 17 points a game—that was a big, big swing.

LEACH: And he became SEC Player of the Year. He understood the game so well in terms of the little things he did beyond knocking down an open shot. You can speak to that as a player and a coach.

PRATT: What he did for that team besides the defense and hitting the open shots, he got the paint touches. He was able to split the pick and roll, the dribble handoff. He was able to split people, to get by people. And then there's Murray. He's averaging 20 a game, getting good looks because Ulis had pulled the defense in. Derek Willis at times got good looks. Briscoe was up and down from the perimeter but Ulis, by being able to go places with the ball, wherever he wanted to go off the bounce, he created for others. I think that's how that team got by that year.

LEACH: One of the low points was a loss to Ohio State in the CBS Classic in Brooklyn and that spoke to a theory you have from your playing and coaching days about the upcoming Christmas break.

PRATT: They were just going through the motions. They wanted to go home for Christmas. It's the "getaway game," and players aren't always focused on the opponent at hand. But that loss and the one at UCLA showed a little bit about what you might think about this team going forward. They didn't think they needed to be clicking on all cylinders, but they did. They had one pro guy on the team, Murray. Then a bunch of scrappers who, when they didn't scrap and fight, they weren't going to win. They weren't overly talented.

LEACH: One of the season's most talked-about moments came after they beat Louisville [75-73] in Rupp in the game right after that stinker in Brooklyn. That was eight wins for Cal in nine tries against Pitino. And as Pitino is walking off the court, a fan snaps a picture of him flipping off some UK fans who were getting on him.

PRATT: He acted like he didn't do it but I think he was frustrated and it was a close game and they had a really good team. He was frustrated and he reacted the way many people from the East Coast do with one-finger salute and that was it. Of course they tried to backpedal, but he did it. Everybody made a big deal about it, but I thought he was just frustrated. I've been frustrated as a coach.

LEACH: But just own it.

PRATT: He did not own it. It was a highlight of that game. It was a hell of a close game. There's always woofing before the UKU of L game, always. It was a hell of a ballgame between really good teams.

LEACH: That Kentucky team never strung together a long streak of wins. There were some tough beats, too, especially the one at Kansas where they played really well against a really good Kansas team. One of the few times, I remember: at the end of regulation they ran a play between Ulis and Murray and they didn't execute it well, one of the few times that happened between the two of them. They didn't get the shot at the end of regulation and then Kansas ended up beating them in the overtime. Really, really good game. So they were a team that could hang in there with a really good team like Kansas on the road, but sometimes teams have flaws. If it's a personnel thing, where you need a five man and you don't have it, sometimes you can't fix that. Now, if your flaw is that you're just inexperienced, maybe you can come out of that like the 2014 team overcame that as the year progressed, especially late. But if there's something you're missing and don't have a way to get it, eventually it's going bite you. And that's what happened to that team.

PRATT: To your point, the Kansas game and the Tennessee game both back to back, on the road. Kansas was ranked fourth and Kentucky 20th, and they played a helluva game. I remember that play. Ulis came down and was set for Murray to, as Ulis attacked the left side of the Kansas zone—it was right in front of us. Murray was supposed to slide to the corner. Instead he stayed at the wing and Ulis made the bounce pass because the defense pulled up on him. He reacted when they pushed out on him—he threw the bounce pass thinking Murray was going to go, or Murray didn't think he was going to go or made a decision not to go. The ball went out of bounds and it went to OT. That place was rocking! Unbelievable atmosphere.

LEACH: There was another tough beat down at Texas A&M. There was a tough call that Isaac Humphries got for slamming the ball down. He did it out of excitement and not any frustration with the official, and he got T'd up and they ended up losing in overtime. That was a really tough loss for them to take.

PRATT: That was a crappy call by that referee. Again, we were right there. They were going from our left to right. Isaac just put the ball down out of excitement, and the referee, it might have been Pat Adams, was trailing and he T'd him up from behind. That was crazy but after that, they went on somewhat of a run. Look at the losses that year. I don't think they had a loss to a ranked team. They lost to unranked teams.

LEACH: With the exception of Kansas. That's an interesting point. What does that tell you? If they're a little bit off, they could lose to anybody?

PRATT: Yes. If they didn't have that fight and scrappiness they were subject to lose to anybody because they didn't have that much offensive firepower. They were a good defensive team. They ran dry offensively sometimes. Particularly if Murray and Ulis didn't have the ball in their hands late in the game to make a crucial play or a crucial shot, they didn't have anybody else who could do that consistently.

LEACH: They had to lean heavily on two guys. Down at Auburn, Derek Willis had a nice game and that was his breakthrough moment to what would turn out to be a good finish to his career the next year.

PRATT: Derek was so up and down until his senior year. I thought he really struggled with his confidence. He couldn't withstand a bad shooting game or a turnover or getting beat on defense. Maybe some of that was Calipari not having a lot of trust in him—or maybe the kid felt Calipari didn't have trust in him, let's put it that way. He never could consistently play with confidence through, let's say, a two- to four-game stretch. He just never put it together that year, but he was able to pull out of it his senior year and finished strong.

LEACH: The last highlight of that season was down in Nashville, in the SEC Tournament title game against A&M, which had a really good team. Murray and Ulis were sensational and they won another SEC Tournament title. It was like two heavyweights in the ring going at it.

PRATT: Danuel House was on that A&M team. He ended up playing in the NBA.

LEACH: Ulis had 30 in that game, 30 points and one turnover in 45 minutes. That's a pretty strong line.

PRATT: He was a ball-dominant guard. That just goes to show you, back to what I said about Ulis from the year before, the 38-1 team: I never thought this guy, coming off that year—I liked him, we appreciated what he did in the 38 and one run—but never would I have imagined that he was going to get 30 points in a game. He could hit the open shots but the next year, he really developed into a guy who could make a play. To get the paint touches, to do the little runner. He was good at stopping and popping too. For him to get 30 in that game, or any game off of the year before, when he was a freshman. Boy, what a swing that was! I mean, how many guys in college do that? Go from averaging three or four points a game to what he accomplished the next year. He was more valuable running the show, defending, really putting pressure on the ball and creating issues defensively. Then all of a sudden the kid pops up and can average 17 a game. Incredible job by him.

LEACH: They go out to Des Moines and win the first one and then they're playing Indiana, which was ranked 14th. Talked to our buddy Don Fischer [IU radio voice] before the game and he was really high on how well Ogugua "OG" Anunoby was playing and how underappreciated he was. He was just the perfect matchup for Murray. He could guard him out on the perimeter and he had the length to bother him and also the length to be able to give him a half step and still be able to deny threes, and that was one of those situations where Indiana had just the right matchup for Kentucky. Murray ended up seven for 18 and only one for nine on threes.

PRATT: I'd watched them during the year and had admired him as far as his defensive capability. You and I talked about him during the broadcast and what he did that game against Murray, who had really gotten good at setting his man up off a pick. He tried to create situations where Poythress ends up low and bring Murray out to the wing, catch, shoot, or pass it inside, or play a two-man game. But to make any of that work, you have to really set your man up off that low block. You got to get him caught; they're either gonna have to switch out on you—then you have a mismatch—or he's gonna go behind or go over the top and you've got the ability to fade to the corner. Ulis was going to get him the ball, so you figured that's how we scored a lot of baskets. Anunoby would fight through that pick, man. I'll never forget that and because I like the kid and then I saw what he did when Kentucky was trying to go to their leading scorer and run some of the things we saw all year, how he really broke that stuff up. That was the difference in the game. His defensive play. They had a big guy.

LEACH: He had 19 points too. For that team, it goes back to if Dakari Johnson had stayed one more year. It would have helped him; I think he would have been a first-round draft pick. You thought that too. And it would have certainly given that team what it needed to go deeper.

PRATT: And Skal wasn't the guy [for the low post].

LEACH: If Dakari had stayed, then Skal could have been more of the guy who he wanted to be.

PRATT: To the Dakari leaving early point, that was just as the

NBA was changing, they still hadn't gone 100 percent with the five-out offense and the three-point shot. They still liked the big, strong guy at the low block. A lot of teams. So if he came back one more year, I think he could have ended up in that first round and made himself some money and stayed awhile.

LEACH: He was one of those examples. Really nice kid and he's done well in China. I'm sure he's doing well financially there and I'm happy for him, but he might have had a shot to stay longer in the NBA had he stayed one more year at Kentucky. I go back to the line you always use about guys needing to understand visiting the NBA versus a chance to stay in the NBA. And I'd forgotten Charles Matthews was on that team and didn't play much, but he goes on to have a nice career for a Michigan team who made a Final Four and he was a guy that would have developed into a nice player at Kentucky.

PRATT: And Matthews at that point in his career, I don't think he was physically tough enough for Cal. He didn't have the right mental attitude to deal with a coach who wants toughminded and physical players. Maybe he got discouraged with that because later on he became a nice ball player. No question about it.

LEACH: He probably would have developed some of the stuff you're talking about with just a little more time.

PRATT: Absolutely. He played for John Beilein [at Michigan]; he is a shooter's coach. Played a lot of that 1-3-1 zone, so it was a little different defensive atmosphere and offensive atmosphere. I don't think Beilein put the physicality and the toughness at the top of his list.

LEACH: Kentucky, had they beaten Indiana, they were then going to play North Carolina in the Sweet 16, and I don't think they could have beaten Carolina. That was the Carolina team that was the national runner-up to Villanova.

PRATT: It was an all perimeter-oriented team. Again, they did well when they scrapped and fought defensively, but they were offensively challenged.

LEACH: That's the last time Kentucky and Indiana played. I think you're with the fans who would like to see that series come back at some point, right?

PRATT: Absolutely, I'd love to see it come back. I didn't grow up in Kentucky, didn't really understand the rivalry. I understood Ohio State and Indiana playing, but when I got to Kentucky I heard my fellow freshmen talk about the Kentucky-Indiana high school all-star series. Casey was my roommate and he would talk about that game and the people he played against and so I got a good feel from those guys, my Kentucky high school teammates, about what that meant to them and how important that rivalry was. It meant a lot so my senior year we played the first game back in that series, which had also stopped. I can't tell you what year it stopped but it had been on hold too, and in December of '69 we played Indiana and started the series again and the next year they opened up that new arena and I think that was Knight's first year. I would like to see it. It makes sense.

LEACH: There are business reasons that get factored in to scheduling but I enjoyed those years when you'd have Indiana, North Carolina, Louisville, three home and homes on successive Saturdays in December. Hopefully it comes back in some way, whether it's neutral courts or home and home. I always enjoyed working games in Assembly Hall, those buildings with a lot of history in them. I think we were told that Indiana had the chance to be in that CBS Sports Classic and turned it down, so they ended up getting Ohio State, and if Indiana was in that thing, it would at least show up occasionally on the schedule, every three years. Kind of like Carolina does.

PRATT: Indiana really blew that, to Ohio State's advantage. That's a good round-robin basketball and gets a lot of coverage. Indiana blew that one.

2017

Calipari's highest-scoring team at Kentucky was this one. With two dynamic guards in DeAaron Fox and Malik Monk leading the way and with Bam Adebayo controlling the lane, it was the kind of team that the BBN would usually be crazy about, but it seemed to take awhile for that embrace to come, perhaps because of losses in marquee games to teams like UCLA and Kansas and then a sorta hard to explain 22-point loss at Florida in early February. But the Wildcats won the rematch with the Gators by 10, and by tournament time, the fans were all in and convinced this Kentucky team had what it took to win it all.

LEACH: They beat Michigan State by 21 at the Garden in the Champions Classic matchup. Monk hit seven threes and led Kentucky and State's big freshman, Miles Bridges, he was a nonfactor but for me, the first "wow" moment was that game Thanksgiving weekend in the Bahamas when they played Arizona State. It's not like ASU was great but it's a power five team and to put up 115 points [115-69] was an eye-opening moment for what this team might be capable of.

PRATT: That game was very interesting because we played it in a ballroom. I didn't think the lighting was the greatest and we just shot the hell out of the ball. [*laughter*]

LEACH: Of course, then they came back and lost to UCLA. It may have been you telling me this or maybe it was Cal—yes, it was Cal—before the game UCLA really thought they had a chance to win because they either flew in early or they flew charter, which Pac 12 teams typically don't do. So they went to the extra expense to get themselves settled in earlier. Cal thought that was an indication that they believed they had a good chance of beating Kentucky. But the next really big win came out in Vegas against North Carolina. It was 103-100, the kind of score you rarely see anymore, and Monk was out of his mind that day.

PRATT: He was hitting them from anywhere and everywhere. Remember, Roy took his sport coat off and threw it down in the end zone when he got all mad. He didn't like the officiating, but his team wasn't playing good defense—and actually neither team was.

LEACH: It was an entertaining game. Like a matchup game from your era.

PRATT: Yeah. They had a couple like that. The UCLA game was a lot like that too. Old-school basketball. [UCLA won 97-92.]

LEACH: Kentucky and Carolina both shot over 50 percent. One team had 10 turnovers; one team had nine. Two good teams that played at a really high level. The Cats came back from that trip and lost to Louisville. They were off that day for whatever reason.

PRATT: Louisville was ranked 10 and Kentucky was six and it was at Louisville. The Wildcats didn't have the usual hop to their step. That was right before Christmas too, and I would bet they were feeling pretty good about themselves. Three-game winning streak beat North Carolina with a clutch shot by Monk, then they roll into Louisville—not taking anything away from Louisville, but I don't think they were the same team.

LEACH: They went through a stretch at the end of January when they lost three out of four and it was nearly four in a row except for Monk saving them with a late bucket to get them to overtime at home against Georgia. That team that we had seen in the Bahamas at their best now looked like they were going south. What do you think happened?

PRATT: Didn't the shooting kind of leave us at that point? Bam wasn't Bam yet. Monk and Fox struggled to make some shots. They were so dependent for most of the season until late, on their perimeter shooting. Bam really came on in February. He started hitting the elbow and short corner. He became a factor. Briscoe was in and out on his shooting during that stretch and he was starting at the other forward with Derek Willis.

LEACH: They won the rematch with Florida in late February by 10 and started to find their groove. Most of Cal's teams won with their defense, but I thought that team won more with offense.

PRATT: I would agree. And Bam really started putting it all together, playing at both ends of the floor instead of just one end, just the defensive end. He learned how to stay out of foul trouble. He was a factor at both ends of the floor for February, March.

LEACH: He went through a stretch, to your point, where he had a stretch of 10 straight double-figure games and 11 out of the last 12 down the stretch, so it was a glimpse of what we are now seeing in the NBA. How surprised are you that he has evolved into the player that he has in the NBA?

PRATT: Only at the offensive end. I knew the kid was a bigtime defender. He was going to defend in that league. I knew he could score around the basket. What I didn't anticipate was his ability to move out on the floor and become a stretch four or stretch five. We didn't see that at Kentucky because obviously, they didn't need it. They had Monk and Fox and Briscoe and Willis. That was, as you said, maybe Cal's best offensive team. They had some guys on the perimeter that could shoot it.

LEACH: Fox got going at the end of the year when he went back home to Texas; he had a big game against A&M, scored 19, got his Whataburgers that he loved for the postgame meal. Then he played lights out when he came into the postseason. He really started to hit his stride. He had 20 in the SEC Tournament—in fact, he had two 20-point games. Had the 39-point game in the NCAA Tournament against UCLA and really settled in and played well. He had a nice run at the end of that season.

PRATT: Fox was a prototype point guard. He had speed and quickness to beat you off the bounce, get to the paint, create for other people, and he had the people on the outside could knock down the open shot because he shrunk the defense so much. Man, he had some quick hands, didn't he?

LEACH: As fans know, a lot of guys don't stay four years anymore, and Dom [Dominique Hawkins] and Derek did that. Two Kentucky guys that fans embraced because of that. They got to see them grow over four years. It was like it used to be. I was happy to see Dominique play so well that he made the All Tournament team as a reserve. Played great in Nashville. If you'd have had an All Smile team, he would have been on it. Great teammate, great leader, and a winner.

PRATT: He had some big plays in the NCAA tournament too. Played with a lot of confidence. Calipari had a lot of confidence in him. And then Willis started doing things besides shooting. Started doing a better job defensively. Cal left him in longer because he would rebound and do things defensively. Most coaches, if you do those things, they are going to let you play a little longer. Both of those guys had struggled at times, but because they were Kentucky kids, fans wanted them to play more. There's always a controversy around a Kentucky kid but boy, when they had their chance that season, they took advantage of it.

LEACH: They go into the NCAA, have a tough second-round game against a good Wichita State team. Kentucky didn't shoot it well but survived. That was one of those games that showed how that team had grown because they had a game where they didn't shoot it well like that stretch back in January, and this was a game where they were able to beat a good team without shooting well because they had grown defensively and I remember thinking,

"That's the kind of game you need to win to get to a Final Four," and a rematch with North Carolina is what ended up denying them that opportunity.

PRATT: If you look at both those teams, Carolina had some good guards, experienced guards; Joel Berry II was a veteran. They had good bigs. Hell, they won the championship. Kentucky was right there with them. We knew what we had with Monk and Fox once we saw them playing, but Bam came on strong—and then another thing, Briscoe and Willis fit that team because Briscoe could drive it and do some things, either score it or pass it off the bounce, and Willis could go to the corner and get ready for a shot, and then Bam just kind of opened it up for everybody defensively. I've always said, if that Kentucky team beats Carolina, they win the national championship.

LEACH: It's a game that should have been played in the Final Four instead of Elite Eight. They should not have been in the same region.

PRATT: No question. Calipari brought that up a couple of times.

LEACH: For all the controversy about the officiating—and I didn't think it was very good in the first half, but it was both ways. But in the second half, it ended up being a game that the players decided, as it should be. There were two plays where Kentucky defended Carolina really well, got them down right to the end of the shot clock and Theo Pinson hit a shot right ahead of the shot clock buzzer and then Justin Jackson hit one and both of those plays, either one or both of those, if they miss the shot and you get the rebound, Kentucky probably wins, but it was two players for UNC who hit two big shots. Two big baskets right at the end. Kentucky defended the whole possession really well, and those are kind of back breakers when they still score on you.

PRATT: That's what Roy Williams's teams do. He doesn't want to slow it down. He wants to push it and he wants to get as many possessions and get as many shots up as possible. That's the way he was at Kansas. Solid defensively but the real gear for them is fast and that's what they did and that's why they were so damn dangerous. They could make the big shots like you just talked about.

LEACH: Roy's teams train to maximize possessions so they fast-break even after made baskets. Most teams don't do that, and so Kentucky makes a basket to tie it and Carolina, it's not just a lucky play, it's the way they are trained to play, to immediately race back down the court after a made basket.

PRATT: And it was the first time maybe that we had seen a team that just loved to keep the ball alive on the glass by tipping it back, particularly on the foul shot. It's all geared to getting those extra possessions, and they'll tip it back and the players know, so they station themselves in situations where they can get the rebound. That's a smart play and they had a few of those in that second half.

LEACH: Such a tough beat for a team that had really grown. They needed to win by their offense early, but by the end of the year they could also win with their defense. They grew into a team that could have easily won the championship.

PRATT: Something interesting happened after that game. All the team buses pulled in under the arena. So, I'm standing, we're standing outside the bus waiting for everyone postgame. They had the food out for the players and us, and I'm just standing there. Carolina's bus was across from ours, maybe two football fields away. All of a sudden, here comes Roy Williams. We've been friends over the years, and he comes over and says, "Mike, that was one helluva basketball game," and I said, "Roy, you're right. Your kids played well. Our kids played well." Then he said, "Yeah, it's a shame somebody had to lose but you guys have nothing to be ashamed of. You played really well." He was very complimentary. Then he walked back to his bus. I always thought that was big of him to see me standing there and come over, and he was just worn out. I could tell he was just exhausted. Some of the UK staff was standing around wondering, "What the hell is he doing over here?" That was nice of him.

2018

The overlooked guy in a highly touted class of recruits ended up being the one who led the way for this team: Shai Gilgeous-Alexander. The buzz about his game started in the summer before the season. That kind of hype is often inaccurate, but this time it was on the mark. Yet the team's season never quite seemed to take flight. They had a blowout win over an unranked Louisville team and their best win was a good one, over seventh-ranked West Virginia, but at one point, this team lost six of nine games, including four in a row. They played arguably their best game of the year in beating number 13 Tennessee for the SEC Tournament title but then lost 61-58 to a very average Kansas State team in the Sweet 16, when a path to a Final Four trip had fallen into their laps due to some upset losses elsewhere in the bracket.

LEACH: Looking back, it's kinda funny that you had several guys who are still in the NBA on a team that is not remembered as being anything special. Kevin Knox was the highest-rated recruit coming in, but you had Hamidou Diallo who has done well in the league and Shai is a rising star. PJ looks to have a bright future and Nick Richards was on that team too. And Wenyen Gabriel has been on an NBA roster too.

PRATT: The guy who grew the most out of that team was Gilgeous-Alexander. Knox played as you expected, more of a finesse player, and PJ struggled with the freshman stuff to figure out who he really was. Hami struggled with his shooting. He just never seemed to want to be there. He's one of those guys that if he had his choice, he thought he should be playing in the NBA. I thought defensively it was not a typical Calipari team. I just didn't think the total team defense was typical. If I remember correctly, they were not a very good road team.

LEACH: The one exception to that was the win at West Virginia, which was ranked seventh at the time. They fall behind 15 at the half and rally to win behind Knox's 34 points [still the biggest rally from a halftime deficit in the Calipari era]. But they lost to UCLA in New Orleans. Lost at South Carolina, at Tennessee, at Missouri, at A&M, at Auburn, at Florida. You're right. So when you see that in a team, does it tell you something about their mental toughness for postseason?

PRATT: It tells you a lot about their ability to focus. I don't think it's necessarily toughness as much as it is about the ability to focus, and that comes with an inexperienced team. Sometimes when you start losing like than on the road and you're looking down at a couple more you go, "Damn. I don't like playing on the road."

LEACH: They won four in a row in late February, but three of those are at home. Then they lose to Florida but then they go out to the SEC Tournament and win it. Wenyen had the huge game against Alabama [seven for seven on three-pointers], and then Shai had a Shai day against Tennessee in the finals—30 points, seven boards.

PRATT: I never had high hopes for this team either in the SEC Tournament or the NCAA Tournament because they were so erratic. You and I talked about it. Then we win the SEC Tournament and we go out to Boise, Idaho, but I didn't have a whole lot of confidence in them, and then we beat Davidson. Arizona is upset, which would have been our second opponent, and they were loaded with talent. I thought we would have had a really hard time with them. So then we get Buffalo, who was an offensive juggernaut at that time with the three-pointer, and we win that game. Then all of a sudden the whole bracket opened up.

LEACH: Kansas State, Nevada, Loyola Chicago in the other half in Atlanta.

PRATT: So, you go, "Maybe I misjudged this team."

LEACH: I don't think it's misjudging; I think they got breaks. The bracket opened up. It looked like they had a shot to get to a Final Four very unexpectedly, but some of the flaws in the team showed back up in terms of they weren't quite able to take advantage of that opportunity.

PRATT: They probably thought Kansas State on paper wasn't quite that impressive. Obviously, Loyola beat them the next game. But they were unranked, and Kentucky was a top 20 team and I think they overlooked Kansas State.

LEACH: You know, that may go back to what you were saying about being so young and the road game losses showed that inability to focus, so maybe that showed up in that situation.

PRATT: I think so. You go into Atlanta and there's all the media and they read about Kansas State—they're not impressed. Those young kids are never impressed.

LEACH: And everybody is already penciling them in to the Final Four, not only in Kentucky but nationally too. That team doesn't have veterans to say, "Let's get focused" or just the types of personalities. Shai was a quiet guy, Knox was quiet. They're pretty much all freshmen.

PRATT: PJ was somewhat quiet too. He blossomed into a terrific leader the next year. I thought Hamidou always had one foot out the door. Quade Green, I never knew what to make of him. Was he a two, was he a one?

LEACH: Nice kid. Remember, he got the eye scratch and had the sunglasses, patch, and he came out and you interviewed him, I think after Virginia Tech—he had a big game. He could be a really fun kid to talk to.

PRATT: He was a bright kid and could easily converse and we joked about the patch.

LEACH: And he cut up with the fans. You see now what they went on and did. You think, maybe if they had a couple of older guys to mix in with them, it might have been a better team.

PRATT: I think so because you had one guy you could count on to make big plays late in the game off the bounce and that was Shai. Then, of course, Knox wanted to catch and shoot. He wasn't a power player. PJ just battled block to block so it was a struggle offensively for this team.

LEACH: The Kansas State game, they did a nice job on Shai. They knew he was the straw that stirred the drink for Kentucky. Then, it was a little of a sign of what was to become for PJ because he played lights out in that game but he couldn't make a free throw. He was playing so hard and so well. He was so dejected on the podium after the game. The player we saw that night was the player he grew to be the next year.

PRATT: I think you're right. PJ, in that game, had a nice first half but he just took over the game in the second half.

LEACH: They could not guard him. He had that move where he would face up on a defender maybe eight to 10 feet from the basket and then he scored facing up and turn and back a defender down. Tough for opposing bigs to guard a guy like that.

PRATT: Talking to people after the game, a lot of them were bitching about his foul shots but I said, "Yeah. I think if you sat down with that kid, he didn't know why he missed them either, but who else was battling inside? Nobody." Knox wasn't. Hamidou wasn't. They weren't willing to mix it up. PJ took that game over in the second half, and I thought if he could overcome the missed foul shots mentally, he would become a really good player the next year. And he did.

2019

Another trip to the Bahamas in the preseason boosted the optimism for this team, especially with Tyler Herro getting off to a fast start down there with his shooting. But the optimism derailed in the opener with a 34-point loss to Duke and Zion Williamson. An incredible defensive performance by Ashton Hagans sparked the Cats to a convincing win over a top 10 North Carolina team in Chicago and that steadied the ship. The SEC was really strong that year, with teams like Tennessee, Auburn, and LSU all being ranked. There was some drama with PJ Washington's foot injury in the postseason, but they put themselves in position to make it back to a Final Four. The old saying is that it is a guards' game in March, and Auburn's guards carried the day in Kansas City and led the Tigers to an upset of Kentucky. We were all thinking it would be a rematch between Kentucky and Duke in the Final Four, but neither team ended up making it there.

PRATT: That kind of beatdown was a shock. I think I told you at the time that I wondered how long it would take them to bounce back from that. When they beat Carolina on a neutral floor and then won at Louisville, they were starting to come out of it.

LEACH: They had a nice win over a top 10 Kansas team in the Big 12/SEC Challenge game at Rupp. Kentucky had three double-doubles in that game with PJ, Reid Travis, and Keldon Johnson. They really defended well, out-rebounded Kansas by 13. That was an example of that team at its best. In the conference, the two games against Tennessee were interesting in that Kentucky won big at home and then lost by 19 down in Knoxville. Tennessee won the rubber match in the SEC Tournament. It was only the second time UK had ever lost in that round of the tournament. This time it was very close, a four-point win for the Vols, and PJ came out of that game with a foot injury that sidelined him for the first two games of the NCAA Tournament.

PRATT: Grant Williams and Admiral Schofield were a tough matchup for Kentucky throughout their careers. Maybe the name "Kentucky" inspired them. They played hard every time. Tennessee was really good, and the crowd for that game was like a regional game in the NCAA. Great atmosphere.

LEACH: As far as I understood it about PJ, the doctors told UK the best hope was to put the foot in that boot and having him take his weight off of it and that was the best chance for whatever the injury was to heal—but they wouldn't know for sure until the boot came off more than a week later. That turned out to be right before they were going to play Houston in the Sweet 16. Fans got annoyed at Calipari for how he talked about the injury, but I remember I was sitting at midcourt at the game day shootaround for the Houston game and Cal still wasn't sure if he was going to PJ or not and how much he'd be able to play if he did go. As it turned out, PJ played 26 minutes, scored 16 points and had a late block that helped to win the game for Kentucky. I certainly was surprised because I thought PJ was a really fierce competitor.

PRATT: He made really big plays. He was a go-to guy. Cal could trust him to make a play defensively or offensively. The year before he missed a bunch of free throws [in a tournament loss to Kansas State], and he could have let that bother him, but he did not. He's on my list of guys that you'd want to get the ball at the end of a game. He really refined his back-to-the-basket game. He had some serious moves and he could stretch the offense by facing up and shooting the trey. And his toughness defensively was there both years.

LEACH: I thought that Auburn game was scary because they had "that look" that you see teams get when they're on a run late in the season, like that UConn team with Kemba Walker. Auburn had those veteran guards and they were oozing confidence. Kentucky blowing them out in Lexington was flukish because the Cats hit a bunch of threes. The two-point win down at Auburn was more indicative of how the teams stacked up, but I wonder if some players didn't fully appreciate how tough the game was going to be. That was the first year that the NCAA allowed team broadcasters to watch practices, and the game day shootaround was not as sharp as I'm sure Cal would have liked. What do you remember about that game?

PRATT: Kentucky did a helluva job guarding the thee-point shot, but they were 12 of 21 on free throws. I thought it would be a tough matchup because sometimes they'd have four guards on the floor and three all the time. They wanted to push the ball and they were aggressive defensively, pushing and holding. The little point guard Jared Harper was really good. Defensively, he tried to overplay and shake the ball loose and that bothered Ashton Hagans [seven turnovers in that game]. I thought Bruce Pearl's whole offense revolved around paint touches and kick out for the trey. They wanted to trade threes for twos.

LEACH: Auburn was in the top 10 early in the year when they played Duke in Maui so that was a highly regarded Auburn team. Do you think the Kentucky players didn't take the Tigers as seriously as they should because they had beaten them convincingly in February at Rupp?

PRATT: No, I just think Kentucky had a bad night at the free-throw line. One more foul shot and there's no overtime.

LEACH: From '17 through the 2020 season, all of those teams had a realistic shot at getting UK back to a Final Four. But this one in '19 I didn't think was good as the '17 group, which to me was the best of those four seasons.

PRATT: I thought the '17 team was the best of those. In '19, with PJ playing as well as he did, I thought they were the second best [of that group].

LEACH: This 2019 season reminded me of that 2005 year we talked about earlier. Not an overpowering team but playing their best basketball at the right time and you could compare PJ as a leader and tough guy to Chuck Hayes, and they unfortunately ran into another team that was hot at the end of the season. This team lost in overtime and that '05 team lost in double OT.

PRATT: That's a good comparison. PJ was an anchor [like Chuck Hayes was on earlier UK teams].

2020

It was quite an up-and-down start to that season with a win over Michigan State in the opener and a shocking loss to Evansville a week later. But the Cats found themselves when they beat Louisville after Christmas, with only three losses the rest of the way and some really good wins, like the one in overtime at Texas Tech. And when they rallied from 17 down at Florida to win on Montgomery's last-second tip and did it without their starting point guard, we had the sense that this was a team well positioned to make a run at the Final Four in a season without any dominant teams.

PRATT: That team had seen the highs and lows and they had figured out who they were. I thought they were going to make a good run. Their confidence level was really high, and the other thing you felt about them was if they got to the charity stripe, they were going to convert. They were playing together, and I thought they could do the little things that can help you win a tight game, the kind of game you're going to have to win to make a run. They had nice balance, four players in double figures, and that was a heckuva rebounding team. They really were playing with a lot of confidence. Cal had a tight rotation of eight guys. That team was primed going into the SEC Tournament, and I think they were set up for the next step. If you believe that guards win NCAA Tournament games, I thought they had three really good guards. And then Nick was the eraser and rebounder. I'm not sure anybody else had that combination. Clutch guys at the guard spot who could get to the line and convert and that's always big in the tournament. That was a Final Four–caliber team.

LEACH: Immanuel Quickley was a cool story out of that season. So-so freshman year but always worked hard. There were a few flashes of what he would become in this second year, but he lost his confidence along the way in year one. Calipari was really working on that confidence in the lead-up to the games in Kansas City for the regional. He kept telling him about what they called the Sam Cassell "big balls" dance. Fans can Google it; the thing actually traces back to the movie *Major League* and the Pedro Cerrano character. Anyway, it's about a player's confidence, and Calipari kept using that to try and connect with Quickley, to get him to believe in himself. It eventually happened in this 2020 season and boy, was it fun to watch.

PRATT: When you fight through it adversity] like Quickley did, you grow and become less hesitant and fearless. Quickley loved to get fouled. He wasn't afraid to take a shot. The year before, he was playing hesitant. He wasn't hitting his shots; he was making some turnovers and he wasn't playing a lot. I remember that shootaround the day of the Auburn game; Calipari was really trying to pump him up because he knew he would need Quickley to play in the game against their three guards.

LEACH: When you and I would talk about players that season, I remember that you always thought Quickley was not getting enough attention as an NBA prospect, and you told me you thought he'd have a long career in the league.

PRATT: I did. The reason was that he played to his strengths. He had the runner, a stop-and-pop game that he was very confident in. He was a really intelligent player, and guys like that who know what their strengths are will always do well. He had a toughness about him.

LEACH: If Quickley had not won SEC Player of the Year honors, Nick Richards would have. And I can't imagine the odds you could have gotten on something like that after Nick's first two seasons. What clicked for him in that third year?

PRATT: I think he felt more comfortable playing. Some players have a tendency to not do things instinctively—maybe you're afraid of being taken out, or the fans will get on you, or they'll write about you. I think Nick just played ball. Previously, he was hesitant and now all of sudden he had a flow to his game.

LEACH: I thought Assistant Coach Kenny Payne did some of his best work in helping develop Nick into the player he became in that third year. You don't get to see players develop like that over time much anymore.

PRATT: Nick wanted to be a player. I'm not sure he had ever been taught how to play until he got with Kenny. Kenny helped him learn how to play the game and when Nick learned, he got better and better. And it gave him more confidence.

LEACH: That team had players that could rise to the big moment. Nick was dominant late in that Louisville win, when Kentucky was coming off a two-game losing streak and really needed a win. And thanks to Nick they got it against a top five team. And remember the game that Tyrese Maxey had in his debut, in the Champions Classic against a Michigan State team that was ranked number one.

PRATT: I didn't know what to expect from him, and he put on a show. Cassius Winston was supposed to be all-world and Maxey just ate his lunch. It was quite a start, especially being at Madison Square Garden.

LEACH: How surprised were you about Johnny Juzang and EJ Montgomery leaving?

PRATT: They said Johnny was homesick. Maybe he was, but I hated to see him leave. When you've been in a program a year, you know the lay of the land. Why would you leave if they signed a couple of guys that play your position? I think he gained Calipari's trust, so that one really hurt. Johnny struggled defensively at times, but he could make some hoops. And EJ, physically he wasn't ready for the pros. His toughness level wasn't high enough then, but he could have gotten there. You can't play at that next level without some kind of physicality. I wonder how much EJ really loved basketball. I don't know that, but I wonder.

2021

Whenever there's a disappointing season, some fans will usually ask if we were glad to see the season end. That's never yet been the case. We love doing the games and we love the time we spend together—along with producer extraordinaire Jim Barnhart—as a broadcast team for games, practices, meals, and everything else, and we're always disappointed when a season is over. But with that said, this year was certainly not as much fun as the other ones. The saving grace was that at least the Wildcats made almost every game interesting. Broadcasters hate blowouts, and in almost all of the losses, the outcome was in doubt in the final four minutes—it's just that this team struggled to close out games, which is something Calipari's teams usually do very well. The pandemic presented unique challenges, such as doing all nonhome games from a studio created at Memorial Coliseum and spending hardly any time around the players, to get to know them better and share some of their personalities with the fans. That proved especially disappointing when the news came about Terrence Clarke's tragic death.

PRATT: Nineteen years old is just way too young. When I was in college, I remember losing three former teammates from high school in Vietnam; one of them I was really close to. It happened in my sophomore and junior years at Kentucky and I remember clearly thinking, "They're my age and now they're gone." It gives you an empty feeling in your stomach. That was really hard on me.

LEACH: It was clear to see that Terrence's teammates got the same kind of gut punch you did when this news filtered back to Lexington.

PRATT: He seemed to be a very happy kid, enjoyed life. It's so sad.

LEACH: This pandemic took a tremendous toll on everyone, but those players had not only that isolation to deal with like the rest of us, they endured the loss of teammates [Clarke and Ben Jordan, a player on the 2020 team who died in January] and the burden of failing to perform up to expectations that are always the highest at a program like UK's. As you said, we did not get to know these particular players all that well, but it's easy to appreciate how difficult the season was for them and we'll probably never fully appreciate the mental toll it took on them.

PRATT: Who knows what goes on with a team when you start 1-6? I never had that happen. I can only imagine the mental issues. I don't think anybody could have saved that team after that start. When the pieces don't fit, you're going to have some issues—issues that can't be corrected quickly—when guys have games that don't complement each other.

LEACH: In a typical year, you and I would see them practice multiple times before the start of the season, but everything was understandably locked down tight because of the pandemic and trying to keep everyone healthy. Therefore, your first chance to see the team play together was in the first game, and after they had played a few times, I remember you telling me that you didn't think the pieces fit well together for that team.

PRATT: I just didn't see the complementary play. There were a lot of guys that looked similar—tall, lanky, long arms—and played alike. And then they had "ball stoppers." As I watched it play out into December, those ball stoppers, once they tried to make their own play, everybody else stood around and watched them. That limited the people involved in the offense and if guys are standing around, they're less likely to rebound. And they couldn't stay between their man and the basket. You saw it early against Richmond and it turned out to be a problem they had for most of the year. Cal's best teams were teams that had a mix of guys like Monk and Fox, who figured out if they came and played hard and the way Cal wanted, they were going to get drafted and make their money. They didn't get out of their comfort zone and try to prove anything to NBA scouts. They just did what they did best and what they were asked to do. There were others like that, but I'm just looking at some stats for those two. Some guys come to Kentucky with an attitude that "I'm a one-and-done," but what they miss is that NBA scouts watch every Kentucky game. You can't try to be something you're not.

LEACH: I worked a few games with Sam Bowie in the 2000 season when Ralph had some throat issues he was dealing with and he told me an interesting story. Sam was trying to help Jamaal Magloire get on the right track and he would tell him to stop taking those 15-footers that Jamaal liked to shoot, to show the NBA scouts that there was more to his game than he had shown. Sam told him about Horace Grant focusing on his role as a rebounder and how Grant fashioned a long and lucrative NBA career with some great Chicago Bulls teams by doing one thing well. Sam told Jamaal to showcase what he did best and not what he did not.

PRATT: That's such a good story. Some guys get it, some guys don't. Most of them are going to be "rotation" players in the NBA.

LEACH: This team had such a problem closing out games. In the portion after the last TV timeout, around the four-minute mark, they were frequently in good position and then they made plays that lost those games rather than plays that could have won them.

PRATT: I think part of the issue was that they didn't have a true point guard. They had a couple of guys that were disguised as point guards that were really wings. At the position, you look for people who can make a shot or create offense for others. That led to more ball-stopping situations because we didn't have somebody who could grab the bull by the horns at the point.

LEACH: As this season played out, I remembered the line Jeff Van Note used to use when talking about his NFL days with a lot of bad teams in Atlanta—"Winning is a habit and so is losing."

PRATT: That is really a true statement. And having too many ball-stoppers out there early led to not getting enough people involved in the offense at crunch time. The offensive rebounds are typical of a Calipari team and we didn't get that, and I think a lot of that comes from having a stagnant offense and we were very stagnant early.

LEACH: Calipari tried to get Cade Cunningham and then also recruited Sharife Cooper. Do you think a true point guard would have been the key to keep what happened from happening?

PRATT: Oh, if they had gotten Cunningham, yes. But family always trumps anything else. [Cunningham signed with Oklahoma State, where his brother was on the staff.] Typically, a Calipari team relies on size and length and being more athletic than other teams. They were very good on the boards, particularly offensive, and he had a ball handler or two who could create space for themselves and others. Now, we had a team that was his worst of his teams in effective field goal percentage, second worst in turnover rate, third worst in offensive rebounding, and worst in the rate of getting to the charity stripe. They struggled to score at the rim, and he talked a lot about they couldn't finish through contact, so they ended up taking a lot of two-point shots and didn't hit 'em. They couldn't finish at the rim, struggled with the midrange shot, and they were shooting a lot of threes early and the offense just broke down.

LEACH: In discussing 2013, you thought Ryan Harrow struggled with a more physical brand of play in the SEC versus the ACC. Did you think that caused problems for Olivier Sarr too?

PRATT: I do. Carolina has been physical lately but outside of that, the teams in that league are more finesse teams. The SEC is more physical defensively.

LEACH: There were moments when you thought they were going to break through, like when they beat Florida convincingly in Gainesville and when they whipped LSU in Rupp, but they took steps back both times. But that week when they stayed in Tennessee because of the weather and won a close one at Vandy and then just blitzed Tennessee, it felt like the people around the team thought a breakthrough might finally be happening. I remember their game day shootaround was really good, and that's often a good sign, but when they lost to Florida, making some of the same late-game mistakes they had so many times in earlier losses, it felt like that was kinda the last straw.

PRATT: It's like they reverted back to what they did in November and December. Playing not to lose instead of playing to win. That's how teams play when they're losing. You become tentative, your confidence is shaky, and I think that's how they played for most of the year, after that 1-6 start.

LEACH: Dontaie Allen was a significant storyline during this season. A Mr. Basketball from Kentucky with a rep as a bigtime scorer, and a lot of fans clamored for him to play more on a team that was struggling offensively. From everything I could tell, Calipari really likes Dontaie because he works hard, and he didn't get on social media during that time and say anything to stir things up. My sense was Cal respected the young man's effort and that's part of why he came back to him late in the year. Dontaie struggled frequently on defense, but he can improve that, and I like his instincts for passing and for getting defensive rebounds, so I think there's more there than just catch-and-shoot.

PRATT: I think fans hurt this kid [with that pressure]. He was coming off a redshirt year and an injury. I don't think he fully understood how hard the games were going to be, especially once he had some success. The best thing that happened to him was that 23-point game at Mississippi State—and that was also the worst thing that happened to him. By the end of the season, I think he had a much better feel for the game. He cut harder, he worked at the defensive end. He seems like a good kid, and anybody that scores 50 points in a high school game, I'm interested in. I was excited to hear the news about him coming back. I would have been very disappointed if he had left, like I was with Johnny Juzang.

LEACH: I know some fans expressed concern about Calipari being stuck in his ways and they worried about him making changes, but whether it was roster makeup, coaching staff, style of play, I never had any doubts that he would shake some things up because he is such a fierce competitor. And you've known him a lot longer than I have.

PRATT: It can be a great story [to turn things around]. I'm pulling for him as a former player and I know other guys are too. We have pride in this program, and I know Calipari does too. For whatever reasons he shuffled his staff, and I'm sure he spent a lot of time reevaluating what he did. Look, all coaches will tell you they don't care what anybody says, but coaches want to be loved just like all of us. Cal is a bright guy and he's competitive as hell. People that don't think he's focused on a national championship are crazy. All of sudden, he is starting to talk about the effects of the G-League and the transfer pool, and I think this is going to give him a chance to recalibrate his thought process. We'll see changes—maybe some, maybe a lot. But I know this year tore him up. I think he's going to look at fewer ball-stoppers and more guys that can create for others. People think it's all about the three-point shot, but you watch the Zags and Baylor, they were balanced. I think the game has swung to offense. You have to have a team that plays together and then it's rebounding. Baylor just lit Gonzaga up on the glass. And you've got to be solid defensively—if you're better than that, great.

LEACH: Kentucky's struggles led to a lot of discussion about style of play. The phrase "modern basketball" got tossed around a lot. How do you think the game is changing and how will Kentucky find its path in that area?

PRATT: You have to be in transition. If you do, the defense will lose guys in that style and when they do, if it's a three-point shooter, you're getting a wide-open shot. But for me, it goes back to a balance that this Kentucky didn't have. Everybody packed in their defense against us and the big guys had a hard time getting the ball where they needed to get it. I really think that transition game is going to be so important. I think the game is going offense first, then rebounding, and then defense. You have to be solid defensively, to create some turnovers and some ill-advised shots, then you take it and push it up the floor.

LEACH: Calipari has had to adapt to different types of teams, and he embraced that from the start here at UK. He's always believed in having his teams defend at a high level, and they have won many different ways on offense. 2011 relied heavily on the threes; 2017 was an offense-first team because of the firepower he had. On the final radio show last season, Calipari talked about the way the game was changing and that you might have to sacrifice some on the defensive end in order to get some other skills on the court offensively. It's fair to question why he didn't come to that thought sooner, but it's also fair to point out that he had teams just a play or two away from a Final Four in '17, in '19, and maybe in '20. How do you think he'll adapt as we move forward?

PRATT: No coaches want to hear all of the advice from the fans or the media. They're all thin-skinned and they don't want to be forced into doing something. But I think Cal will change and find the right pieces for his philosophy. In practice, Calipari is always saying, "Push the ball, push the ball."

LEACH: I think it will be harder to have many guys on the floor that can't make three-point shots.

PRATT: I agree. You can have a guy like that if you have the right people around them, but I don't think you can have more than one non-shooter. It's putting the pieces together. All you want is guys that can hit open shots. The college game may look like the NBA game, but that's the best of the best. They do things differently and better than college teams. I think in college, you have to score in transition by using the trey.

LEACH: You often use a phrase "family, friends, and fools" in talking about what sometimes drives poor decisions about players going pro or changing teams. Will the tremendous increase in transfers change any of this dynamic?

PRATT: I think there are a lot of unhappy guys in that portal, so you have to be careful. They can mess your locker room up. Coaches aren't going to tell a kid to stay or go because it can hurt their recruiting. Every team in the Final Four had at least one transfer. The key is to keep some guys around an extra year or third if you can, like Nick Richards, and blend in these guys that come from quality programs like the kid [Kellan Grady] from Davidson. You know he's been well coached. You look for guys that can add to your team, including in the locker room. That pond of the one-and-done's was full of fish when Calipari started, but more and more people started fishing in that pond. In today's game, do you think you could get three guys of the quality of Wall, Cousins, and Bledsoe? No way! It makes it harder to build your team with guys that you have to polish, and are they going to give you the time you need to polish them? It's tough now for those reasons. I think it's going to be hard to have a back-to-back champion now. There's going to be a lot of talk about roster management, which really means you're going to have to get lucky with your roster.

MEMORABLE CHARACTERS

Players and coaches understandably get most of the attention, but there are many people under the umbrella of supporting personnel who make the University of Kentucky basketball program work so well. Here a few stories about our relationships with them.

George Hukle

Hukle was equipment manager under Adolph Rupp.

PRATT: One of the finest guys I ever met. He was as tight as Adolph and Bernie Shively. He counted every sock and every T-shirt. He packed everything for us—all we had to do was show up and head to the airport. We were responsible for our sport coat and tie to travel. "Uke" counted everything—and, to be honest, our practice stuff, you wouldn't want to steal it. It was so bad, holes in things. Uke used to darn socks. But he was a special bird. He was probably in his 60s, retired from the post office, and was just a wonderful man.

To get a second pair of shoes, you had to sweet-talk Uke. I was going home for the summer and I wanted a pair of shoes to play in. He had stuff stored everywhere and he gave me a pair of these shoes that we [the players] had tried and didn't like. They tore up my feet. [So Mike took his case to his head coach.] I know Uke is pissed off at me for bringing the Baron down there for a pair of shoes. Adolph said, "Give me a new pair of shoes," and we're talking about Chuck Taylors [the Converse model of the day]. Uke looked at me with that look in his eye and said, "I hope you have a great summer, you pissant." It's funny what you remember.

Uke traveled with us and kept assists. Kentucky was one of the few schools that kept assists, and Casey and I used to kid him about Issel scoring 100 points and we're getting three assists. Everybody who played had special memories of George Hukle.

Bill Keightley

Keightley was the legendary UK men's basketball equipment manager.

LEACH: "Mr. Wildcat" had served under Hukle, with both of them working for the postal service. And Joe Hall was so good at improving the marketing of the program that he helped make Bill into a favorite "character" in the Kentucky program. Bill lived and died UK basketball and everybody, including opposing coaches, loved him. If you were an opposing coach coming in to play the Wildcats, you wanted to meet Bill and Cawood Ledford.

PRATT: He hit it off with Uke so well and Uke groomed him. They both were the perfect guy for the job they had. I remember a trainer told me that after we lost to Ohio State Uke was over in the corner crying. Those two guys were synonymous with the program.

LEACH: In his role as equipment manager, Bill also oversaw the managers for the team and that was a special relationship.

PRATT: They loved Keightley and loved his stories. They ask me about things he had told them. He imparted his Kentucky basketball history on those managers. And nobody works harder than the managers. And so many of them have gone into coaching. Keightley was a father figure, to put an arm around them if they had a bad day. They truly loved the guy.

LEACH: In the years working with Tubby and then Billy, the

pregame interview was usually done at the pregame meal, four hours before tipoff time. I'd get there early and often it was just me and Mr. Wildcat. I had known him from covering the team as a reporter for WVLK and the UK Network, and he made me very so welcome in this new role. The other thing I remember is that the two things we most often talked about were two of his passions—the Cincinnati Reds and high school basketball in Kentucky. Bill would have never said anything to a coach about who they recruited, but suffice to say no one was a bigger Chris Lofton fan than Mr. Wildcat. He mentioned that one to me a few times.

Van Florence

Florence was leader of the 101 Club, aka the Blue Coats.

PRATT: Van had a heart as big as all outdoors. He ran that club and it's a great bunch of guys, very selfless. He got to know everybody, from the wealthiest people to the everyday fans. He was very close to Pitino and to Tubby. Van was a special guy.

LEACH: On road trips, Van, Bill Keightley, and Bob Wiggins [who had a long record of consecutive UK games attended] were the three amigos. There was no "bull session" more fun to be a part of than talking basketball with those guys.

Adrian "Odie" Smith

Smith was a member of the 1958 "Fiddlin' Five" national title team.

PRATT: Odie was very close with Van and with Tubby too. He could tell some stories. Such a nice guy. And talk about a guy that could shoot. He never tried to tell anybody what to do or how to do it. He was just there to offer support, a guy that had played there.

LEACH: I'm sure the players had no idea the caliber of player Odie was in the NBA. Won the all-star game MVP in 1966 and, last I heard, he still had the car he was given for the title by *Sport* magazine. Odie worked for Fifth-Third Bank in Cincinnati and had access to some really good tickets for the Reds' games, so I'd make a point to go to a game or two with Odie every summer—and we'd usually make our way up to the broadcast booth to visit with Marty Brennaman. He and Odie were great friends.

PRATT: That's how I remember Odie, when he was with the Cincinnati Royals.

Mike Casey

This chapter has been about nonplayers, but we can't do this book without talking about the Casey/Pratt friendship.

PRATT: After we were done playing, we did a lot of things together. Played golf quite often. We'd go up to Keeneland. I remember when he brought his daughter Laura down to show me. We just had a lot of things in common. We'd tailgate at the football games and growing up in Kentucky, everybody knew him. He was such a legend. He was born to play at Kentucky.

LEACH: It was a treat for me to get to know him through you. I remember a dinner in Atlanta on the eve of the SEC Tournament. You, Casey, and Jim LeMaster were holding court, telling stories about Coach Rupp and Coach Lancaster. The rest of us would have bought tickets to listen. And as a young Kentucky fan, I remember hearing the news about Casey being in a bad car accident the summer before your guys' senior season. I know a lot of Big Blue fans believe having Casey would have been the extra push you guys needed to win the title in 1970.

PRATT: I remember getting the call about Casey being in a bad accident. When you start with somebody, you have common ground. We were together four years, and the first one was a freshman-only team. It was like a piece of you was taken out. We had some good players to step in, but it wasn't the same. We did some things that we don't anybody to write out. Those will be left untold. I miss him a lot. He listened to the radio and on the way home, I'd get his call, right around Frankfort. His name would pop up and he would critique the game from there to Louisville, what I said and what I should have said.

LEACH: There are a couple of stories involving Casey that you must tell. Let's start with the one about getting your prime rib taken away before even having a chance to cut into it.

PRATT: It was after a loss at Florida. One side of Alligator Alley [where the Gators played] was all windows and all this light came in. We played the noon game and we were ranked high and they upset us. We get on the plane to go to Georgia and the flight was canceled so we went back to the hotel. We had eaten breakfast at eight in the morning, the game was at noon, and we didn't get to go on the plane, where they had a box lunch for us after the game. So we go back to the hotel and we get a call that it's time to eat. So Casey and I go down and we were one of the last ones to get there. We had not yet been served when Adolph and Harry walked in and Harry was smoking that Chesterfield [cigarette]. Adolph asks the trainer what we're eating and it was prime rib and all of sudden, Harry says, "Hagan, Ramsey, and Tsioropoulos [the famous trio of All-Americans from the 1950s] ate moon pies and RC Colas. These boys played like a bunch of turds today and I don't know why we feed them anything." Adolph listened and then he told the trainer, "Put the boys to bed." So we all go back to our room—and we get a call about two hours later and they had ordered hamburgers and some milk.

LEACH: Now, my favorite story about you and Casey. He has a 30-plus point night in a game at Memorial Coliseum and afterward, Coach Rupp is telling Cawood about how sick Casey was before the game—or at least, that's what Coach Rupp thought was the case.

PRATT: Tickets were hard to get. There was a door that led you to the underbelly of the Coliseum, and we'd let our friends in and then they'd just find a place to stand and watch the game. That night I've got these guys on hold, waiting to come in, and Casey is coughing and that was the signal that Adolph was there. I hear Adolph talking to him and Casey says, "Coach, I'm sick and I'm just out here getting some fresh air." You would have thought the guy was on his deathbed and all he was doing was watching for Adolph. We get calls after the game from people who heard the radio show asking, "How's Casey feeling?" And the trainer called me to ask about him and I said, "Forget about it. He's fine."

BEST OF THE WILDCATS (AND MORE)

Favorite games during our tenure

The 2012 national title win over Kansas is the automatic number one for both of us.

Pratt

2011   59-57 v. Princeton in opening round of NCAA Tournament. "Kentucky was a four-seed, and the way they won that game against a Princeton that you're in trouble when you fall behind, that was a huge game."

2011   The regional wins over Ohio State and North Carolina. "Kentucky was the underdog in both games so that was impressive."

2010   64-61 win over UConn in Madison Square Garden. "I thought that sent a statement to college basketball about Kentucky in Calipari's first year."

2014   78-76 win over #1 seed Wichita State.

2019   Kentucky beats #1 Tennessee by 17. "The old rivalry of Kentucky and Tennessee, and the crowd was amazing."

2006   #23 UK over #4 Louisville 73-61. "The game was dominated by Rondo and led UK to an unexpected win."

Leach

2011   Kentucky beats #1 Ohio State 62-60. "Getting to do a Kentucky game in the Final Four was always a dream when I first thought about wanting to have this job, and when they beat that Ohio State team that night in Newark, I was convinced it was going to happen—and it did. We were staying in an awful hotel in which the TVs in the rooms didn't even get ESPN, so we were all watching the coverage of UK's win in the hotel bar at about two in the morning, and I saw the big smile on the face of Josh Harrelson's dad when the anchors were talking about his son. That was a cool moment to witness, thinking about how my own dad might have felt in a moment like that."

2012   Kentucky beats Louisville to go to the national title game. "It was the first time two archrivals like that met in a Final Four game, and Kentucky winning meant we were going to get to work a national championship game."

2001   Tayshaun Prince hitting five straight threes to start the game against North Carolina. "Certainly one of the loudest times I've ever heard in Rupp was when he hit the fifth one from just a couple of steps across midcourt."

1999   Kentucky beats Louisville 76–46. "Ralph Hacker called me the morning of the game to say he was having throat issues and for me to be on standby. Ironically, the same thing had happened for the previous year's U of L game, but Ralph was able to push through. This time he couldn't, so I called my first Kentucky basketball game. I didn't know if there were ever be another one, so that one will always be special for me."

2014   Kentucky beats Wisconsin on Aaron Harrison's third consecutive game-winning shot. "Play by play, you hope to get one moment like that in a tournament run, and there were three in a row; this one put UK into the title game for the second time in three years.

Best individual single-game performance in a big game

Pratt

2002   Prince's five consecutive three-pointers v. UNC in December 2001.

2002   Prince's 41 points v. Tulsa in NCAA Tournament.

2009   Jodie Meeks's 54-point game at Tennessee and also his 46-point game at Freedom Hall against App State (which broke Pratt's record for most points by a Kentucky player at Freedom Hall).

2010   Wall's 25 points against UConn in Madison Square Garden.

2017   Monk's 47 points v. UNC in Las Vegas.

2017   Fox's 39 points v. UCLA in Sweet 16. "He was out for blood against Lonzo Ball."

2011   Knight's 30 points v. West Virginia in round of 32 game in NCAA.

2016   Kevin Knox's 34 points v. West Virginia in Big 12/SEC Challenge

Leach

2015   Karl-Anthony Towns's 25 points v. Notre Dame in Elite Eight. "The undefeated season was in real danger and the team would have missed out on a Final Four, but Kentucky kept going to Towns and he delivered every time."

2011   Josh Harrelson's 17 points, 10 rebounds, and three blocks against Ohio State All-American Jared Sullinger.

2005   Patrick Sparks's 25 points to lead Kentucky past Louisville 60-58 at Freedom Hall. "The Cats were down 32-16 at halftime. Sparks caught fire in the second half and then hit three free throws in the final seconds to go from one to two up."

2017   Fox's 39 points against Lonzo Ball and UCLA in Sweet 16. "With the stakes for a game at that spot in the tournament, he was unguardable."

2012   Anthony Davis's 18 points, 14 boards, and five blocks to lead UK past U of L and into the title game.

Best pure shooters

Pratt

You can put these in any order you want—Meeks, Monk, Murray, Herro, Lamb, and then I can't make up my mind between Hawkins, Sparks, Willis, and Aaron Harrison.

Leach

Meeks, Devin Booker, Murray, Lamb, Quickley—that's my top five, but it was tough to leave Monk and Herro out.

Most underappreciated players

Pratt

"Jorts" (Josh Harrelson), Kelenna Azubuike, Gerald Fitch, Darius Miller, Patrick Sparks

Leach

Julius Randle (one double-double from tying Issel's school record of 25 in 1970), Keith Bogans, PJ Washington, Deandre Liggins, Patrick Patterson, Erik Daniels

Game on the line—who do you want to take the last shot?

Pratt

Prince, Bogans, Monk, Sparks, Knight, Fitch

Leach

Towns, Aaron Harrison, Prince, Monk, Meeks

"Glue guys"

Pratt

Chuck Hayes, Darius Miller, Patrick Sparks, Michael Kidd-Gilchrist, Gerald Fitch, PJ Washington

Leach

Chuck Hayes, Deandre Liggins, MKG, Tyler Ulis, PJ Washington—that's my starting five for the "glue team" with Ramel Bradley and Darius Miller off the bench

Best opposing player performance v. UK

Tom and Mike conferred to come up with a list of some of the most impressive performances by opposing players in a game against Kentucky.

1. Chris Lofton, Tennessee, 2006: 31 points by former Mason County High School star in Vols's 75-67 win at Rupp; not the highest-scoring game by an opposing player, but given it was against the home state school that did not recruit him, that said a lot about his competitiveness.

2. Cleanthony Early, Wichita State, 2014: 31 points; a valiant performance in defeat in a game in which both teams played at an ultra-high level offensively; this one ranks above higher-scoring games because of the NCAA Tourney stage.

3. Elston Turner Jr., Texas A&M, 2013: one of only three players since 1971 to score 40 or more in a game at UK—enough said.

4. Jay Williams, Duke, 2001: 38 points including seven threes in an overtime win v. UK at the Meadowlands.

5. (tie) Corey Allmond, Sam Houston State, 2009, and Bubba Parham, VMI, 2018: Allmond had 37 points with 11 threes v. a fourth-ranked UK team at Rupp; Parham scored 35 v. 10th-ranked UK at Rupp and had 10 three-pointers.

Favorite arenas we've worked in (outside of Rupp Arena)

Pratt

Madison Square Garden. "For me, it was the mecca of college basketball when I was growing up."

The United Center

Dean Smith Center, UNC

Pete Maravich Assembly Center, LSU

Thompson-Boling Arena, Tennessee

Leach

Madison Square Garden. "I grew up as a Knicks fan and loved Walt Frazier, so the first time I worked a game at courtside at the Garden, when UK beat UConn in December 2009, was quite a memorable moment."

Allen Fieldhouse, Kansas

Athletic and Convocation Center, Notre Dame "I remembered watching on TV when Notre Dame ended UCLA's 88-game win streak, and I wanted to go to that spot on the floor when Dwight Clay hit the shot."

Pauley Pavilion, UCLA

Lahaina Civic Center, Maui. "Nothing better than walking out after a doing a game and seeing the Pacific Ocean."

Best road game restaurant

Pratt

Ariccia, the Hotel at Auburn University

Louisiana Lagniappe, Baton Rouge

Pat's Steakhouse, Louisville

Rosebud, Chicago

City Grocery, Oxford, MS

Dreamland, Tuscaloosa, AL

Leach

Spencer's for Steaks and Chops, Omaha, NE. "Side story on this one is when UK ticket manager Joe Sharpe, a true "foodie," was in the travel party. Joe scoped out many great eating spots and knew this one was famous for its strawberry shortcake. Some of us conspired with the waiter to tell him they had run out of shortcakes and he was crushed—and mad. Such a funny moment when he got the real story—and their steaks were fabulous."

Rama Jama Cafe, Tuscaloosa, AL. "Right next to the football stadium and full of Alabama football history."

Graycliff Hotel & Restaurant, Nassau, the Bahamas. "Hat tip to Bob and Mary Nutter for finding this gem."

St. Elmo's Steakhouse, Indianapolis

Pat's Steakhouse, Louisville

Biscuit Love, Nashville

Best postgame interviewee
(for Mike Pratt's postgame shows)

Jamal Murray, Tyrese Maxey, Keith Bogans, Darius Miller, PJ Washington

ACKNOWLEDGMENTS

WHAT A RUN this broadcast team has been on for 20 years. We have had courtside seats and the privilege of covering so many highs of Kentucky basketball—plus a few lows. When I first took this job, I felt it would be a great opportunity to reconnect with old friends and make new one in BBN. Tubby Smith was coaching at that time, and we had a relationship from back in the day. He always made me feel very comfortable. I have enjoyed my relationship with all three UK coaches during our time, and I thank them for being so cooperative. I could not have gone 20 years without the total support of my wife Marcia, our blended family, and our friends. Marcia has developed into as big a Cat fan as there is, and as with all relating to BBN, she shares her thoughts on that with me. Tip of the hat to my daughter Tamaryn for her recommendation to take the job because "TV is a young person's world and you will look good on the radio." That from a Mizz Broadcast Journalism major!

A big thank-you to all my teammates who have followed the broadcast and shared their thoughts with me. I've always felt that in a way I represented them also doing the radio show. Thanks also to one of my closest friends in this world, the late Mike Casey. He always helped me with his insight, either on a golf course or on my drives back to Louisville after a game. This guy was born to wear the UK Blue. I miss him dearly!

The glue for this broadcast team has been Jim Barnhart, our producer, who has kept us on the air through some difficult spots. Mike Dodson, our executive producer, has always been my go-to guy for UK basketball and football history. JMI, the rights holder

Acknowledgments

for the UK broadcasts, have been wonderful to work for. They have put together a successful team and allowed me to be a part of that.

Many thanks to Brooks Downing, Larry Ivy, and Jim Host for convincing me to leave FoxSportsSouth to do UKBB radio network., and to Mitch Barnhart and the entire Athletics Department for their terrific assistance during this run. I am grateful for the friendship of many fans, with a special mention to the late Van Florence, Bill Keightley, and the 101 Club.

Cawood Ledford, Ralph Hacker, Kyle Macy, and Sam Bowie left us a legendary radio network and I hope that can be said of our tenure. To Joe B. Hall, thank you for coming to Dayton Ohio and convincing me to attend UK.

To BBN everywhere, I hope you have enjoyed this run as much as I have and thank you for being so kind and supportive of our broadcast team.

—Mike Pratt

It's hard to believe this is the 20th year of our UK Radio Network men's basketball broadcast team. Mike called in the summer of 2020 to suggest the idea of doing a book together, and it's turned into a fun project to relive so many good times doing jobs we enjoy so much. Most of the thank-yous below pertain primarily to UK basketball since this book is about the time Mike and I spent together doing games. One of these days, Jeff Piecoro and I will do a project like this for UK football, and there will be numerous other names to list at that time.

The list of people to thank for their help on this book as well as support for the 20-year run starts with my wife Robyn, an extremely talented news anchor for WLEX-TV who stepped away from that job to focus on our two children, Connor and Caroline. That proved to be a wise decision as both are talented, caring young people of whom we are tremendously proud. And Robyn transcribed most of the interview sessions Mike and I did for this book and gave me some good advice along the way about how to make it better.

Acknowledgments

As for the work life, let's start with our producer Jim Barnhart. He not only gets and keeps us on the air but he's our go-to guy for computer and iPhone issues (he's that guy for John Calipari, too, by the way). We have great times on the road trips during the season, eating together and watching games and practices. Ditto for our former executive producer, Mike Dodson, who would assist with home games, oversee logistics for road trips, and keep us laughing with some great stories. Thanks also to Tim Ansted of IHeart, who produces our broadcasts from the studios in Lexington and can handle whatever curve is thrown his way—like a power outage in the Bahamas' arena in 2018 that shifted our broadcast to a phone.

A big thank-you to our JMI family, the holder of the media rights for UK Sports. Rather than list all of the folks there who support us and risk leaving somebody's name out, we'll just say thanks to all of them. It's more than just a job for them because they are Wildcat fans like those of you reading this.

Ralph Hacker and Jim Host deserve special mention. I didn't fully appreciate how narrow my career goal target was in wanting to land one specific play-by-play job, but the best part of my plan to accomplish it was wanting to land a spot on Ralph's team at WVLK. That was the flagship station for the UK games in 1984 when I was hired, and working for Ralph gave me insight and knowledge about radio and this career path to a level that I can't completely quantify. It was a wonderful family to be a part of for 16 memorable years. And Jim hired me to join the UK Network on the postgame coverage in 1989 and later promoted me to play-by-play roles. Like Ralph, he gave me valuable advice on how to do this job at the level set by those who preceded me. Both were like father figures in that they could give me constructive criticism and yet I always knew—and know—they have my back. And Jim has been a partner along with my lifelong friend J. C. Faulkner in Tom Leach Productions, which produces my daily *Leach Report* statewide radio show, which helps pay the bills when there are not any UK basketball and football games to work.

Acknowledgments

We also should certainly acknowledge the wonderful friendship and support from UK Athletics. It starts with the ADs—C. M. Newton, then Larry Ivy, and now Mitch Barnhart. There's a great commitment to professionalism and setting high standards within the various sports, and that extends to our network. And we could not do our jobs without the help of the sports information staff. Eric Lindsey and Deb Moore are wonderful assets, and the same goes for all those who preceded them during our tenure. And we sincerely appreciate the cooperation of the coaches and players with whom we've worked. They have always given us the access we needed to do our jobs.

I think back to when I first started in the radio business as a cocky 16-year old in Paris, Kentucky, at WBGR. Bill Brown owned the station, having moved into the ownership game after working as a reporter at one of the top stations in Los Angeles, covering, among other stories, the Charles Manson trial. My first two bosses as operations managers were Doug Vaughn and Jon Darryle Marsh. When I go back and listen to my tapes from those days, I am eternally grateful that I was even hired, much less coached into some desperately needed improvement. And Cawood Ledford was a great influence on me, first just from listening to him but later for giving me valuable critiques on my work.

I'm blessed to have a wonderful network of friends, many of whom go back to my high school and even elementary school days. Again, I won't list them for fear of leaving off someone's name, but they have always cheered me on along this path to calling the UK games, and I appreciate their support more than I can express.

Finally, a big thank-you to the BBN. The high standards of Wildcat fans push us to do our jobs at the highest level of which we are capable. It's an honor for us to sit in these seats and do broadcasts for an audience so passionate about the Wildcats.

—*Tom Leach*